Vanessa Jones

HOW DID THAT HAPPEN?

Understanding Adult ADHD Through Stories of Lived Experience

Wider Perspectives Publishing ¤ 2023 ¤ Hampton Roads, Va

Cover Design by Gretchen Bedell

Illustrated by Hannah Thomas

Many thanks to the Fred Rogers Institute for permission to reproduce the song "What Do You Do?"

US Copyright number pending
1st run complete in December 2023
Wider Perspectives Publishing, Hampton Roads, Va.
ISBN 978-1-952773-84-6

To my parents, for always believing in my capabilities,
and for reminding me to take out the recycling.

Contents

Introduction

I just got off an overnight boat trip in 95-degree heat. My brain is still gently bobbing up and down in my skull and the rooms in my house seem to be rocking. It's a little hard to focus when my brain is bobbing and my house is rocking. In my head I'm not quite on land, and I'm not on the water either. Try having a conversation with me or asking me to do something for you, or pointing out that I just put the pizza in the cabinet, and chances are I might not be entirely with you. Because I am here, in this non-land, non-water, bobbing place that I can't control. Welcome to my home. I have ADHD.

…and I'm a teacher
…and I'm on summer break
…and I really did go on that boat trip
…and I have painted my mud room, power washed my deck, traveled to every major U.S. city, and in short done everything I possibly could do this summer to avoid the one thing I should be doing: lesson plans.
…and now I'm writing this book. Wow, am I ever going to be behind come September!

At the age of 42, when I was diagnosed with ADHD, I did my due diligence and ordered some books on the topic. I read about adult ADHD; I read up on how ADHD affects relationships and work. Though I definitely recognized myself as disorganized and procrastinating, I was in denial about my diagnosis for a long time. I became confused because my experiences didn't totally match up with the official list of symptoms. Or at least, I wasn't sure they did.

The official diagnostic criteria include 18 symptoms of ADHD separated into two categories: Inattention, and Hyperactivity/Impulsivity. It was easy for me to point to the symptoms that weren't mine as a way to deny that I really did have a problem, or if I did it was so mild I could easily overcome it through sheer force of will. I could admit that my desk was a mess and that I'm not good with time management:

Often has difficulty organizing tasks and activities (e.g. difficulty managing sequential tasks; difficulty keeping materials and belongings in order; messy, disorganized work; has poor time management; fails to meet deadlines).

But other parts of the diagnostic criteria didn't seem to fit. For example, I almost never lose things:

Often loses things necessary for tasks or activities (e.g. school materials, pencils, books, tools, wallets, keys, paperwork, eyeglasses, mobile telephones).[1]

I spent a lot of time telling myself "I'm not like that. I don't do those things. I don't have those problems." Yet, I was the one who had finally sought a diagnosis after a presenter in my teaching certification progam revealed some of his struggles with ADHD, and I thought to myself "I'm like that. I have those problems."

---

[1] Diagnostic and Statistical Manual of Mental Disorders Criteria for Attention-Deficit/Hyperactivity Disorder (ADHD) in Barkley, Russel *Taking Charge of Adult ADHD* (269).

I do my darndest to make a plan and to have some control over my life, and yet something unseen generally slows me down or completely derails me. Either I can't motivate myself or I go off in a completely different direction, or I become utterly overwhelmed and stuck. It's like the way I was held hostage by mosquitoes with my partner, Ben, in the cabin of his motorboat. After a nice dinner on the river, we motored to a quiet section of the river where the water was calm, turned on our safety light, and anchored for the night. In the cabin, we had an air mattress and all our essentials. Ben had taped screens over the portholes so that we could have fresh air and not have to worry about bugs getting in. We went to sleep lulled by the gentle rocking of the boat on the water. But peace was short-lived. We woke to the whining of mosquitoes in our ears. A screen had come loose from the top porthole, and mosquitoes were pouring in. He pressed the screen back in place, but it was too late. Mosquitoes were everywhere. In the darkness, we could hear and feel them. We frantically and ineffectively began clapping at the air.

"Get a light!" Ben shouted as he reached for his cell phone. We each turned on our phone lights and held them aloft in one hand while smashing mosquitoes against the walls of the cabin with the other hand. We could hear other mosquitoes outside the screens. They were still coming in through tiny gaps. "We have to shut the portholes," I said as we leapt about smashing insect bodies full of our blood into the walls. We shut the portholes and continued killing mosquitoes until, finally, we lay down exhausted and full of bites in the stifling hot cabin. There was no escape from this place. We hadn't thought to bring insect repellent, and if we opened the cabin doors to weigh anchor and get out of there, we'd be eaten alive before we could get away. Something practically invisible was dictating our experience, holding us back, keeping us from peace and sleep, rattling our thinking and judgment, distracting us every which way.

The fact is, the symptoms of ADHD are wide-ranging and sometimes appear contradictory. Depending on our brain make-up, we may experience more of one kind of symptom than another. However, we have some critical things in common: Most of us have a persistent sense that something invisible is holding us back. We are coping rather than thriving. We want to be more in control, but somehow we're not. We are sure we have great potential, but we're still waiting to reach it. We have always known we were different, that we didn't quite "fit in" with our peers. We have problems doing what we need to do and instead we go after things that are more stimulating and rewarding in the short term. We are disorganized and bad at planning. We have a hard time following through. We have a tendency to hyperfocus, a state-of-being where our brains become so engaged with a task or activity (especially one that holds high interest) that we lose all awareness of time passing (as well as awareness of the thing we were supposed to be doing).

On the flip side, we pay too much attention to everything and can't prioritize. We have experienced mystifying problems with relationships. We can't "feel" time, and hence we are chronically running late. We are inconsistent and somewhat unreliable. We forget things. We are driven as if by a motor, internally hyper-aroused, yet we aren't very efficient. We don't have full control over our impulses, and therefore we sometimes say or do things without thinking and land in hot water for poor judgment. Sometimes we feel so overwhelmed that all we want to do is lock ourselves in the bathroom and watch YouTube on the toilet. These difficulties are not character flaws. There is a neurobiological explanation for why we do what we do.

ADHD is a neurodevelopmental disorder: "– that is, a condition that shows up early in life and interrupts or slows normal development of certain physical, emotional, and social skills."[2] It is characterized by differences in development of several brain regions, all of which affect self-regulation at some level.[3] The largest MRI imaging study of its kind, published in The Lancet Psychiatry Journal in 2017, studied the brain volume of more than 3,200 people, ages four to 63 years old, both with and without ADHD. The MRI images of those with ADHD showed reduced activation in brain areas responsible for inhibitory processes, executive functions (organizing,

---

[2] Pera, Gina. *Is It You, Me, or Adult A.D.D? Stopping the Roller Coaster When Someone You Love Has Attention Deficit Disorder*. 1201 Alarm Press, 2008. 36.

[3] Radboud University Nijmegen Medical Centre. "Brain differences in ADHD." ScienceDaily. www.sciencedaily.com/releases/2017/02/170216105919.htm (accessed July 23, 2020). "Besides the caudate nucleus and putamen, for which previous studies have already shown links to ADHD, researchers were able to conclusively link the amygdala, nucleus accumbens and hippocampus to ADHD. The researchers hypothesise that the amygdala is associated with ADHD through its role in regulating emotion, and the nucleus accumbens may be associated with the motivation and emotional problems in ADHD via its role in reward processing. The hippocampus' role in the disorder might act through its involvement in motivation and emotion."

prioritizing, flexibility, self-monitoring, accessing working memory), motivation and decision-making. Multiple areas of the brain where these processes take place were smaller. They showed a reduced volume of gray and white matter and reduced cortical thickness relative to the non-ADHD brain. Also, the synaptic networks in the ADHD brain were *atypical* in their connectivity across regions of the brain. Basically, our brains grow and are wired differently from the majority of our peers. I will talk more at length about brain differences with ADHD in chapter four.

I hope this study offers you some reassurance that you're not just inherently "lazy" or "unambitious" or "unreliable." Throughout this book, I refer to the ADHD-ers as "neurodivergent" and the people without neurodevelopmental challenges as "neurotypical". It was hard for me to decide what terms to use, but I feel like these are the most accurate words for now. On the one hand, I dislike the word "neurotypical" because of its implication that there is one "normal" or "standard" type of brain against which all others are measured. None of us is the same. We all have diverse personalities, experiences, thoughts, and contributions to make to the world. None of our brains looks exactly the same, either. On the other hand, MRI imaging makes clear that the milestones the majority of children tend to reach around the same time, such as learning to talk or to control their impulses, corresponds to a very specific timeline of brain development. In other words, the growth and development of the brain does tend to follow a basic pattern in the majority of people.

Brains that diverge from this "typical" development, where, for example, a part of the brain develops earlier or later than the majority of children in that age group, create different strengths and challenges from people who don't have those developmental differences. This "neurodivergence" isn't necessarily "abnormal". From a human survival standpoint, it makes sense that a variety of ways for the brain to develop evolved (I'll talk more about ADHD-ers as being perfectly suited for the role of hunters later). However, in a cultural context where there are certain basic expectations of children and adults, it's disabling. These cultural expectations include:

- being able to adapt to changes in routines
- being able to focus in class or at work for prolonged periods
- having varied interests typical for one's age
- developing social and organizational skills similar to one's peers
- being able to tolerate some sensory discomfort, such as loud noises, without difficulty[4]

Our cultural expectations form the basis for how school and work environments are structured, often creating challenges for those of us who are "neurodivergent." The systems and processes we must navigate were built on the assumption that we have all developed in each of the above areas relatively equally. But, because one or more of these areas

[4] Villines, Z. (2022, February 3). *What Does Neurotypical, Neurodivergent, and Neurodiverse Mean?* . Medical News Today. Retrieved April 13, 2023, from https://www.medicalnewstoday.com/

may present significant challenges for us, we don't necessarily get the opportunity to show off our strengths. Instead, we experience stress and anxiety trying to function efficiently on a playing field not designed for us.

My ten-year-old son likes to try to go *up* the down escalators. Sometimes in airports he races me, and he runs up the down escalator while I ride up the up escalator. He usually gets to the top first despite the handicap. But he's always much more out of breath. It's a lot more work to get to the same destination. Life with ADHD is a constant race against a down escalator. At first maybe you can keep up OK, but over time, as you gain more and more responsibilities, you start to lose ground, until you're carried more *down* than you are *up*. People call to you from the top of the escalator. They expect you to do your job, honor your commitments, remember your tasks. But they don't know that you are further and further away, and it's getting harder and harder to hear what they want, and even if you could hear it, you're trying so hard just to keep your footing that whatever it is gets lost.

One of the most internationally recognized writers, researchers, and speakers in the field of ADHD is Dr. Russell Barkley. He has spent his career researching and educating the public about ADHD, and his research and theories have added tremendously to our knowledge about the disorder. In fact, he is such a superstar in the ADHD field that practically no one else writes about ADHD without referring to Dr. Barkley's work. I have become such a fan of his efforts to disseminate clear information about ADHD that I have conferred upon him the epithet "Savior of the Scattered."

In his book *Taking Charge of Adult ADHD*, Dr. Barkley writes "In my years of counseling adults with ADHD, I've come to believe that reframing your view of yourself and your life to put ADHD in the picture is in fact among the most crucial changes you can make to master ADHD. It's the only way I know to keep ADHD from running, or ruining, your life."[5] But if you've been diagnosed with ADHD as an adult, how do you do this? How do you hold the door open for your ADHD diagnosis in order to move towards a brighter future when you've lived your whole life totally unaware of the ways it has hijacked your path? How do you learn, remember, and apply your new knowledge of ADHD to yourself?

There are many books to choose from written by clinical psychologists and medical doctors in the field of ADHD research. These books offer strategies for making the most of the ADHD nervous system and they explain why and how our brains experience difficulty. I highly recommend Dr. Barkley's books as well as books by Dr. Edward Hallowell, Gina Pera, and Dr. Ellen Littman. There is a kind of book on ADHD that is in rare supply, however. It's one that combines the research and teaching with full-length stories about real people and their everyday struggles.

---

[5] Barkley, Russell A., and Christine M. Benton. *Taking Charge of Adult ADHD: Proven Strategies to Succeed at Work, at Home, and in Relationships*. The Guilford Press, 2022. 43.

Those of us with ADHD depend heavily on connections with emotions to help us remember and act on things. It's our work-around for the reduced activation of key areas of our brains. If nothing arouses our emotions, we have a much harder time remembering information and details. In most books on ADHD, the stories about real people who have actually experienced the impact of adult ADHD in their lives are condensed into short paragraphs here and there amidst the research and the advice. Relegated to text boxes, these stories lack the round characters and emotional depth we need in order to remember the valuable points they illustrate.

We can read bullet points and informational text all day, but unless we can directly connect it to our lived experiences on a deeper level, the information leaks out almost as soon as it's put in. We need real people (with real names) to tell their stories of real struggles. We can then bear in mind these stories as we examine our own lives and start making connections. Our own stories slowly start making sense in a broader context. After that, we're in a better position to control our own outcomes.

It seemed to me there was a certain kind of book on ADHD that wasn't being written, and it was the one I wanted to read. Finding out how the brain works and labeling each problem area certainly helps increase our self-awareness, but I wanted a book of stories of another person's experiences with adult ADHD in work, family, and relationships, and I wanted those stories each to connect to specific ADHD problem areas with quotations from the experts to validate and explain them. In short, I wanted the exact opposite of the books available. I was looking for stories with snippets of authority rather than authority with snippets of stories. I was also interested in the differences between the ADHD experiences of those assigned male at birth and those assigned female at birth. How do societal assumptions and expectations of gender affect the ways we perceive ourselves and manage our special ADHD issues?

Since I couldn't find this particular book, I decided to write my own. My ex-husband used to poke fun at me when I couldn't seem to get around to something important I had to do, or I pulled everything out of the closet to get rid of things and then left it all sitting there and went to a parade instead, or I began cooking a complicated dinner at 7pm without checking first to see if I had all the ingredients. When I didn't accomplish what I was supposed to accomplish, I was notorious for saying the same excuses, or laments, over and over, and he joked that these phrases of mine could become my epitaphs. I offer these "epitaphs" to you now as chapter titles. These are my stories, but I refuse to allow them to be the end result of my entire life.

Stories can upset, teach, change, guide, and heal. They are markers along the road. If you have been diagnosed with adult ADHD, but you're not entirely clear on how your ADHD impacts your life, or if you think you or a loved one might have ADHD, but you're trying to understand its specific symptoms and the reasons behind them, then this book is for you. This book is also for you if you beat yourself up on a daily basis for the things you struggle to accomplish and you'd like to know that you aren't alone. I hope you find my stories helpful and maybe even transformative. You have the opportunity to take charge of your stories and to write new ones. You may just need the knowledge, motivation, and support to do it.

Adult ADHD has a wide-ranging impact, and it can, frankly, be devastating to people and their relationships. It can also be downright dangerous. In a 2015 Danish study of almost two million people, researchers determined that people with ADHD have a lower life expectancy and are more than twice as likely to die prematurely as those without the disorder.[6] ADHD actually reduces life expectancy by an average of 13 years for those whose ADHD persists into adulthood because ADHD is fraught with risk factors in every phase of life and development: from driving, to peer relationships, to health, to occupation. In addition, the risk of premature death is higher for girls and women with ADHD than it is for boys and men with ADHD. That's a sobering dose of motivation to help us change our own epitaphs before it's too late.

We are in this together, and that is why I use the pronouns "we" and "us" rather than "they" in referring to people with ADHD. Within many of my chapters, I provide quotations and research from ADHD experts so that you can evaluate your own experiences to see how they fall in line with the many symptoms of ADHD. And once you fully embrace

---

[6] The Lancet. "People with ADHD are twice as likely to die prematurely, often due to accidents." ScienceDaily. www.sciencedaily.com/releases/2015/02/150225205834.htm (accessed August 21, 2020).

and understand the effects of ADHD on your life, you can consciously choose how to move forward (preferably not while driving in a vehicle at top speed texting your spouse and balancing a small dog on your lap).

I read a book several years ago, one of the few I actually remember, that struck a deep chord and has stayed with me in many of its details. It was *The Time Traveler's Wife* by Audrey Niffenegger. In this novel, the protagonist has a condition termed "Chrono Displacement Disorder" which causes him to jump randomly around in his own timeline of life with no control over when and where he ends up. His poor wife, who loves him dearly, has to put up with never knowing when he will vanish and for how long, whether he is safe, and if he'll come back again. The time traveler's greatest enemy is time, as one minute he'll be lying comfortably in bed with his wife, and the next minute he'll find himself naked in a parking garage in the middle of the night in the dead of winter several years in the future with no idea how to get home.

Though I don't know what gave Ms. Niffenegger the idea for her novel, for me it's obviously about a man who is afflicted with ADHD. He cannot situate himself solidly in his own present life. His brain leaps wildly around the time/space continuum, and his body follows. He's just not all there. And his wife, God bless her, does the chores and takes care of the kids and keeps things steady when the husband is carried off in time. Dr. Barkley, Savior of the Scattered, actually refers to ADHD as a form of "time blindness" because we don't see, or find it impossible to plan adequately for, the future. Our lives are divided into "now" and "not now." The implications of the future have no effect on us until it's almost too late and we're on a crash course with consequences.

I want to show you the real story of what it's like to live with adult ADHD, how it feels, who it affects, what heartbreak it causes. I want to show you the fun it can spark, as well. I want you to know there are people like you, and I want to help you understand yourself better. Only after you recognize how ADHD infiltrates your life can you work on changing outcomes to your liking. So, in the spirit of self-discovery, I offer you my epitaphs. When I'm dead, I'm probably not going to remember that I'm dead, anyway. I'll keep insisting that I don't remember it happening, and I'll flip-flop restlessly in my grave looking for some stimulation to break up the boredom. I hope my stories can help you identify, accept, and seek help for your ADHD or for your partner or children who may be struggling. We are creative, dynamic individuals, and the world needs us. If only we could control our time-travel.

1

Social Pitfalls and Misperceptions

I've often joked that if I ever got into a relationship with someone like me, we'd have wonderful adventures but our house would be collapsing around us. Neither of us would get around to removing the squirrels from the attic. Somebody would leave the soaker hose on until the basement flooded. I'd forget to pay the electric bill. He'd walk away from water boiling on the stove and get involved in an air hockey match. We'd go on a trip and accidentally leave the door unlocked at which point squatters would move in. Good luck to them. The basement's moldy and the house is on fire.

So I didn't do that. I steered clear of all super creative, super fun, and super flaky individuals. I married a super competent, ambitious, organized, smart man who quickly began working his way up the ladder and became highly successful in his field. For 16 years, we had a life together. He told me what to do and I did it. He told me what to spend and I spent it. He told me what to sign and I signed it. He told me he didn't appreciate me anymore and was disappointed in my lack of ambition, and I believed he was right to feel that way. My super charismatic, compassionate, forgetful self was a disappointment to him. He treated me like an unruly employee. He managed me, until he moved on to a more fulfilling position. People with undiagnosed ADHD are almost twice as likely to end up getting divorced. Unfortunately, I was part of that statistic.

I had no idea I had ADHD. I knew almost nothing about it, only that it had nothing to do with me. ADHD is something they say manifests in children. You don't just "get it" as an adult. If you have adult ADHD, you've always had it, but the criteria for determining ADHD in children tends to fit boys far more than it fits girls. I didn't have problems in school. I never got into trouble. I wasn't constantly on the move and jumping from high places. I was a gifted, straight A student. I graduated from college Magna Cum Laude. I successfully earned a Master's degree. I succeeded in my teaching career. I thought I could focus fine.

Yet as an adult with adult responsibilities, I found it a real struggle to manage everything. There was a stark contrast between my messy, disorganized, procrastinating, late-for-everything, forgetful, and creative brain and my husband's focused, managerial, detail-oriented brain. I wanted to be more mindful of my life, but no matter how hard I tried, my brain was always sliding into in-between, seemingly useless worlds while his brain was busily climbing ladders. The more my husband accused me of not listening to him, not being able to manage the house well enough, not providing enough structure for our child, not caring about his needs, not working hard enough, not having enough life goals, the more depressed, anxious, and self-doubting I became.

Dr. Kathleen Nadeau, a clinical psychologist who specializes in the diagnosis and treatment of ADHD and learning disorders, sees many women who have struggled for years to balance the responsibilities of a job, a home, and child rearing. Women who feel that something isn't quite right often seek help from doctors or therapists who end up diagnosing them with depression and anxiety rather than evaluating them for ADHD. Yet even after years of therapy, the problems haven't gone away.[7] Doctors typically only consider ADHD as a potential diagnosis of an adult experiencing problems *if* the patient experienced significant symptoms from an early age.

The problem is that many girls with ADHD don't show obvious signs during childhood. In fact, children assigned female at birth often have an entirely different expression of ADHD from children assigned male at birth. Boys tend to "act out," externalizing their symptoms by demonstrating rule-breaking behaviors: running, being physically aggressive, or

---

[7] Sigler, Eunice. (2019, October 10) ©1998-2023 WebMD LLC. All rights reserved. *ADHD Looks Different in Women. Here's How – and Why.* *ADDitudemag.com.* https://www.additudemag.com/add-in-women/

acting impulsively in a classroom setting. Girls with ADHD are more likely to be overly chatty and social, or to "space out" and not hear instructions. Sometimes, girls with ADHD lash out with verbal aggression (even bullying behavior) directed at peers or parents. Generally, though, girls are more likely to internalize their symptoms, blaming themselves for their forgetfulness, or coping with disorganization and problems with self-regulation by developing an eating disorder. Because girls are socialized to be "people pleasers," they may work hard to compensate for and mask their inattentiveness and impulsivity to the point where teachers don't recognize it. Unfortunately, masking their struggles takes a huge toll on girls emotionally and physically.

In my upper elementary and middle school years, I spent a good bit of time wandering around the house partly engaging in activities. I picked out some tunes on the piano, got out a sewing project, played with my dolls, ate a snack, watched some TV. Often, I sat on the floor in front of the screen door rocking back and forth with my eyes out of focus until I could imagine the screen with its black metal bars was a jail and I was trapped inside this unfocused world. Careful what you wish for.

My dad used to say it was healthy to spend time not doing much of anything. He didn't see anything wrong with the fact that I rarely settled into something and stuck with it. I loved to read, and I read for hours when I was in the middle of a great book. But I had a terrible time settling down and starting a new book. I thought it was because I hadn't made friends with the new characters yet, but now I see that it was because I was at the whim of whatever grabbed my attention in each moment. A book that hadn't yet engaged me couldn't call loudly enough for me to hear over everything else that was competing for my interest. None of this was a problem for me when I was young, though. I flitted like a butterfly from interesting thing to interesting thing, and I sipped at the joyful nectar of life.

The diagnostic criteria (DSM-5) for girls were recently modified to reflect an understanding of the often later apparent onset of ADHD symptoms in girls. For a diagnosis, symptoms of impairment must be seen by age 12. The middle school years are a time when students receive less academic scaffolding to help them organize their tasks and assignments. There are many more transitions in the school day and more things to remember and process, so it's less easy to cope successfully with difficulties in organization and time management. Also, the onset of puberty seems to have a worsening affect on ADHD symptoms in girls as the estrogen hormone dips and spikes.

One ADHD symptom that tends to show up sooner, however, even when a girl is academically strong, is problems with peer relationships. A ground-breaking ten-year study from the University of California-Berkeley, begun in 1997, tracked the development of 140 girls with ADHD from childhood to adulthood. It found that girls with ADHD experience more peer rejection than boys with ADHD.[8] With a disconnection from what should be a network of peer support, girls internalize their failures and head into adolescence and adulthood at high risk for various kinds of self-destructive behaviors, far more than boys.[9]

Looking back at my childhood through this lens, I do remember significant moments where I stuck out from my peers. I was a bubbly and chatty kid. I was well-spoken with adults and I was insatiably curious about everything. I loved to learn, and that motivation for learning got me easily through school. However, teachers told me I asked too many questions. There were times on field trips where I was the only one engaged in a dialogue with the presenter. I didn't even pick up on how my peers felt about that. I got overly excited and couldn't stop talking, especially when I was passionate about something. I tended to hyperfocus on interesting topics, monopolizing conversations and not really noticing how others were reacting to what I was saying. The thoughts in my head simply spilled out without much filter. I had a tendency to talk too fast and too loudly when I got excited. Also, I was internally restless. I got very uncomfortable with my quieter,

[8] Hinshaw, S.P., Carte, E.T., Fan, D., Jassy, J.S. & owens, E.B. (2007). Neuropsycholological Functioning of Girls with Attention Deficit/Hyperactivity Disorder Followed Prospectively into Adolescence: Evidence for Continuing Deficits? Neuropsychology, 21, 263-73.
[9] Nadeau, Kathleen G. Ph.D., Littman, Ellen B. Ph.D., Quinn, Patricia O, MD. *Understanding Girls with ADHD How They Feel and Why They Do What They Do*, Advantage Books, Washington, DC, 2016, "Forward." Hinshaw, Stephen, Ph.D. pg. xvii

calmer peers. I could sit still physically, but inside I was all abuzz and needed to be talking, engaging, figuring things out, entertaining.

My parents like to tell the story of when I was six years old and they took my older sister and me to Philadelphia. We did a tour of Independence Hall, and the tour guide told us all about the circumstances leading to The Declaration of Independence. When she asked if there were any questions, I raised my hand and started firing off one question after another. A tour group from Nebraska was so impressed with me that afterwards they asked to take my picture. My parents tell this story as evidence of my being a gifted and precocious child, uninhibited and unafraid of the world of adults. And indeed, being gifted is what allowed me to do so well in school, with my ADHD symptoms not really hindering me until much later in my life. However, my lack of inhibition (being unable to or unaware that I should stop myself sometimes from doing or saying things), and my latching onto anything that stimulated my brain and riding it out for all it was worth (regardless of its effect on the rest of the tour group), were probably both undetected symptoms of ADHD.

I have always been hyper-verbal and emotionally excitable. I can get so caught up in my feelings about things or my enthusiasm for a topic that I don't pick up on the feelings and reactions of my peers. As a young person, carried away by my own reactions, I impulsively interrupted and exhibited an emotional intensity that put people off (though it was cute

when I was six). According to Dr. Littman in Understanding Girls with ADHD, "It is difficult for [girls] to distinguish between what seems urgent to them versus what may be important to their peers….they simply may be responding to the impulse of the moment, unable to focus on the feelings of peers at the same time."[10] I have definitely been guilty of this utter lack of awareness, and I've lost friendships in the process. Things that are really important to me become something that should be important to everybody. I can get stuck on a topic or

---

[10] Littman, Ellen B. et al. *Understanding Girls With ADHD*. 87

idea and not be able to let it go until the people around me see it my way. In social situations, I have a very hard time remaining engaged but not domineering, dynamic but not too intense.

Those of us with ADHD are either "on" or "off." There's not really a middle ground. We have an interest-based nervous system, so either we're all in with our interest fired up to maximum, or we're checked out. In my case, in the classroom I was either totally engaged and asking or answering all the questions (utterly oblivious to my effect on others), or I was daydreaming and doodling. I had a tendency to stare at words on the bulletin board and trace the letters over and over again in my mind's eye.

One year, my 9th grade English classroom contained the phrase "The Pen is Mightier Than the Sword" above the chalkboard. Sitting in that classroom daily, I noticed every little detail of those words: the size and shape of the letters, the color, the space they took up above the board, and especially the lack of a big enough space between the words "Pen" and "is." They were crunched together much too tightly. (Get it? Pen is?) That made me laugh inwardly to the exclusion of anything the teacher might have been trying to teach. I paid attention to all sorts of random details, but I didn't really have control over what I paid attention to. I was often clueless and kind of flaky, but because I was a straight "A" student, no one ever saw any red flags.

No one even saw a red flag when two girls ganged up on me in the wrestling room during gym class. The teacher had stepped out of the room and I was trying to practice my backward roll. The two girls got in my face and began speaking to me with a surprising amount of anger and resentment. It caught me completely off-guard as I'd never even spoken to them before. I ended up getting slapped, hard, and running out of the room in tears. There were various complicated factors at play in that exchange, but I'm sure that my obliviousness to my effect on others didn't help the situation.

People with ADHD often experience social isolation when they say the wrong thing or don't pick up on subtle social cues. When an ADHD child gets particularly excited about a topic, they may go on and on about it and miss social cues that others are bored. Or, in an attempt to get more stimulation from a conversation, someone with ADHD might unconsciously provoke their friend into an argument. Also, being easily distracted makes it hard to be a good listener and to pick up on nonverbal cues. Finally, because self-regulation is a problem with ADHD, we tend to say the first thing that comes into our heads, regardless of whether or not it's appropriate in the given situation. Many of us get known as "interrupters" because we can't inhibit our impulse to jump in. Add to all this the fact that people with ADHD are usually late and inconsistent in their dependability, and it's no wonder that good relationships can often be a struggle.

The social girl-world is intricate and full of pitfalls. Girls stake a huge amount of their self-esteem on social acceptance and emotional intimacy. Girls are under immense pressure to be socially skillful, self-controlled, pretty, competitive, yet loyal to the group. Self-control and verbal ninja skills are crucial in a social world where "girls tend to

engage in verbal aggression, gossip, and social exclusion."[11]
The girl who sticks out because she is too enthusiastic, or
unable to let something go, or insistent that everybody do
things her way, can be perceived by others as selfish, bossy, or
controlling.

Unfortunately, we ADHD-ers have trouble monitoring
our behavior and accurately perceiving others' reactions to us.
We also find ourselves compelled to do or say things that may
not be appropriate to the situation or that don't lead where
we'd ultimately like things to go. As a result of these issues,
girls in particular have a tendency to alienate our peers without
meaning to.[12] When this happens, girls can be harsh and
unforgiving. The girls with ADHD either then become the
target of social rejection, or we get neglected, ignored, and left
out. Girls with ADHD are frequently on the receiving end of
teasing, shaming, and "freezing out." This takes a tremendous
toll on our self-image, especially because we often have no idea
why our peers are treating us this way. We internalize this
shame and lack of confidence, carrying the feeling that there's
"something wrong with us" into adulthood.

Weekly faculty meetings with my mostly female
colleagues are a tremendous source of stress for me during the
school year. I teach in a small arts program where we must

---

[11] Understanding Girls with ADHD.

[12] Hinshaw, S.P., Owens, E.B., Sami, N., & Fargeon, S. (2006). Prospective
follow-up of girls with attention-deficit/hyperactivity disorder into
adolescence: Evidence for continuing cross-domain impairment. Journal of
Consulting and Clinical Psychology, 74, 489-499.

constantly make schedule adjustments and create new events. In addition to trying to pay attention to all the details of who needs to do what and when, I'm overwhelmed with all the unwritten rules of social interaction among my peers. I never seem to get it right. I feel just out of step, unable to discern what it is I'm missing.

Luckily, as a kid, my social world wasn't as confusing. I got involved at a young age in the dramatic arts where my overly talkative, enthusiastic, dramatic, loud tendencies were just the normal quirks of a theatre kid. I was generally the center of attention in my group of friends. Even though I monopolized the group, I was entertaining enough that they liked having me around. Kids with ADHD often play the class clown to hide their weak spots

> *Playing the role of entertainer is a way to use a strength to make up for challenges. If it's done at the right time in the right way, this behavior can be a social plus. Kids often find their peers with ADHD to be truly funny – and fun to be around.*[13]

In fact, many actors and comedians also have ADHD. Theatricality is pretty much built into the wiring of many of us.

We must be careful, though, not to go for laughs at the expense of our self esteem. I was the youngest of two, and my older sister has always been brilliant and focused.

---

[13] Understood Team. *Why Some Kids Clown Around in Class.* © Understood for All, Inc. Understood.org. https://www.understood.org/articles/why-kids-play-class-clown

Whenever we played family games that involved recalling facts, trivia, or anything to do with quickly accessing information or working out a problem in my head, I couldn't keep up at all. I knew I was smart, but I couldn't do a word problem to save my life, because the combination of words and numbers derailed me and I couldn't hold onto the multiple components in my memory long enough to work out the problem.

I made up for these weaknesses by making jokes at my own expense. I felt stupid in relation to my sister, and I couldn't understand why things that were so easy for her were so hard for me. My coping strategy was to make fun of myself and to encourage my family to make me the brunt of their jokes. Over time, this slowly eroded my own sense of competence and set up a dynamic for relationships later on where at best it was OK to put me down in a friendly way, and at worst I endured contempt, disrespect, and being treated like a child.

Studies have found that students with ADHD (especially girls) are often terrible at math. In my role as the "family clown," I didn't know that the weaknesses I was trying to hide were really a symptom of my poor **executive functioning**, especially my poor working memory. Executive functions are those mental processes that allow us to organize and manage our thoughts, actions, and emotions in order to initiate, sustain, and complete a task. They also help us to plan, manage, and organize time.

Working memory, an aspect of executive functioning, is responsible for temporarily holding information available for processing. Basically, my brain has a hard drive but no clipboard for temporarily storing data in an easily accessible and rearrangeable way. It can't hold onto more than one or two bits of information at a time. No wonder, then, that I could never do word problems in math such as "If a train is traveling at 100 miles per hour and the railroad crossing is 3 miles away, how long does Doug have to get his stalled car off of the tracks before the train hits him?"

Fast-forward through time to me at 39 years old, still undiagnosed, and little had changed. I was bright, inquisitive, funny, messy, empathetic yet oddly unaware of my impact on others, and making jokes at my own expense to cope with my shortcomings. One day, after 16 years together, my husband Casey told me he was moving out. I felt just like the guy in *The Time Traveler's Wife* – naked and vulnerable in a place I didn't recognize, with no idea how to get home.

2

Missing the Important Details

When I was in third grade, Mrs. Gosnell assigned us to write out all the steps involved in safely crossing the street. I wrote a very thorough guide, all about coming to an intersection, pushing the button on the pole, and waiting for the light to turn red so you could cross. I was an excellent student, and I never got into trouble or had to meet with a teacher. So when Mrs. Gosnell asked me to stay after class to discuss my essay, I was both surprised and worried.

The time came for me to stay after, and I watched everyone leave the room. As each student left, I felt more and more nervous, trapped there for a reason I couldn't fathom. Mrs. Gosnell spoke gently, "Vanessa, I wanted to talk to you about the directions you wrote for crossing the street." Mrs.

Gosnell took a file from her drawer and pulled out my paper. "What you said makes sense, and I can see that it's been working for you, but that's not usually how we explain to others how to cross the street." I didn't know what to say. I had no idea what she meant. I went through the steps again quickly in my head:

1. Stop at the curb
2. Look to your right
3. Check that the light is red
4. Look left and check that the cars are stopped
5. Cross the street

"But that's how you cross the street, isn't it?" I asked, mortified that I'd gotten something wrong.

"You could look at it like that, but what's the other way to cross the street?" Mrs. Gosnell asked. I stared at her. What did she expect me to say? Mrs. Gosnell was waiting. She looked kind, but it didn't help. I felt stupid. Suddenly it occurred to me that there was something I did not know that it seemed everybody else in the world knew. I realized, in that moment, that not everybody saw the world my way. I experienced a crisis of confidence. I'd always prided myself on being an A+ student, yet here was something I couldn't figure out and everybody else could. I had to admit defeat.

"I don't know," I said, tears coming into my eyes. Then Mrs. Gosnell explained how the cars going in the same direction as me had a light above and in front of them that turned green when it was safe to cross the intersection. I was supposed to look at that light, not the one to my right, and move across when the cars going my direction were also going across. She seemed to think all of this was quite obvious. She seemed surprised that I didn't know.

I had never noticed that there was a traffic light in the distance above and in front of me. I had also never noticed the cars that were stopped next to me on the road and started up when it was my turn to cross. How was I supposed to know that? Did everybody but me get some sort of secret guidebook to crossing the street? How could I have missed those things? Part of me wondered if maybe she was wrong. I mean, what about the whole "Look both ways before you cross the street" thing? I looked right, checked for a red light, and then I looked left to be sure the cars were stopped. I did what I'd been told. In Mrs. Gosnell's version, all you did was look straight ahead. It didn't make any sense. My little process paper on how to cross the street was a defining moment in making me realize that I didn't see things the same as other people. My perception of the world was just…different. I didn't notice things that other people seemed to think were pretty obvious, and I couldn't for the life of me figure out how I was supposed to know what they were all seeing.

People with ADHD miss things. Big things. Big heavy things barreling towards us at high speeds. We step out into the middle of the street and those big heavy things suddenly smack into us and knock us off our feet. Sometimes we don't see things even when they're right in front of us. This is partly because we have so much noise in our heads that we're not even aware of, and our senses are turned way up. At any particular moment in time, we might be hyper-attuned to the slightest noise, or to a particular smell, or be so struck by how something looks or feels that we notice nothing else. Important details have a much harder time standing out for us when our senses are pulling in a multitude of other details without a filter. We are at the whim of that sensory input and the feelings it produces in terms of what we end up paying attention to.

As a third grade street-crosser, I had been so focused on those cars zipping past in front of me whenever a red light wasn't holding them back, imagining how they would flatten me if I stepped off the curb into that stream of metal, that nothing else about the traffic pattern (such as the cars idling right next to me) entered my radar. Now, did it really matter that I missed the obvious details considering that I still understood how to cross the street safely? Perhaps not for my third grade self. But my 16 year old self would certainly need to know how the traffic patterns actually worked if I expected to be able to drive.

The fact that we ADHD-ers tune in to whatever details strike a chord in us can sometimes be an asset. Because we can see things that others aren't seeing, we can sometimes be excellent problem-solvers. In my experience, though, the things I miss have mostly been a liability. I miss what coworkers expect of me because I think they want something else. I see people reacting to me with annoyance, but I miss what made them annoyed. I try to follow a set of directions, but I misinterpret what they are telling me to do. I reach over a fence to pet a goat and suddenly we both get electrocuted. How was

I supposed to know that the fence was electrified? (Sure, there was a sign on the fence, but who notices that when there's an adorable goat trotting towards you)?

It was a running joke in my marriage that I routinely missed things Casey thought were crystal clear. I was routinely indignant because somehow he expected me to intuit what to him was completely obvious but to me was completely elusive. Whenever my logic didn't match up with his (and other neurotypical people's) logic, inevitably there were consequences that I wasn't prepared for. I regularly exclaimed to Casey

"HOW WAS I SUPPOSED TO KNOW?" when it became clear to me yet again that he and everybody else was consulting their secret guidebook to the world and it felt incredibly unfair that nobody was sharing it with me.

While Casey was on a business trip plotting in his mind how and when to extract himself from our marriage, my attention was otherwise occupied by a baby mouse. On an early spring day, five months before he and I separated, I pulled my car into the garage, got out, and looked down to see a tiny baby mouse lying on the concrete floor. Despite having had to capture and evict at least four mice from our kitchen in the previous years, I couldn't leave the baby mouse to die, so I put the mouse in a shoebox in the bathroom, (the warmest place in the house), and I googled "How to take care of a baby mouse." The mouse needed a warm, safe environment, food, and care. Though I had many other things to do, I shifted into high gear and abandoned all other projects in favor of the one with the most immediate intensity. I was going to keep that mouse alive, and the challenge of it fired up all my sluggish neurotransmitters.

According to my research, I would need a heating pad, an aquarium, puppy formula (baby formula would do in a pinch), a new paintbrush for feeding drops of formula (an eyedropper would do if not available), Q-tips, and shredded paper. I didn't have all this equipment, so I went out to find it. I was so worried about the mouse and getting its needs met right away, plus I craved the immediate gratification of getting the mouse all set up in its new space. Since I didn't want to be gone long, I only went down the street to the drugstore to pick up the supplies. They didn't have puppy formula, so I bought baby formula even though it wasn't a great choice. They also didn't have any paintbrushes, so I bought an eye dropper. Luckily, I did find an aquarium at the thrift store next to the drugstore. I rushed home, mixed up the food, put on disposable gloves, and picked up the fragile mouse for its first feeding. After it ate, I massaged its stomach with a Q-tip and gently put it into the aquarium.

Over the next week I carefully fed the mouse, which I had named "Beastie." It wasn't thriving, but I kept trying. I learned later that I was feeding it the wrong food in the wrong way. Though my internet research had guided me towards either baby formula or puppy formula, in fact the baby formula was killing the mouse with too much lactose. Also, since I had been using an eyedropper, Beastie was getting the food too fast and was in danger of bloating to death. It would have been better for the mouse to lick one drop at a time off the paintbrush rather than to be inundated with big drops of formula. With every misguided attempt to nourish the mouse, I was making it sicker. Though I suspected that puppy formula would improve Beastie's situation, I couldn't seem to fit in a trip across town to Petsmart to get the right stuff.

When Casey came home from his business trip and found a mouse in an aquarium in the bathroom, he was surprisingly angry about it. "I can't believe you decided to bring a mouse into our house without even telling me about it or asking what I thought," he said.

"But it would have died otherwise. I needed to get it inside. I didn't realize I had to ask your permission," I said.

"You don't have to ask my permission, but it's my house too and you never even bothered to ask me what I thought of the situation. You just stuck a wild mouse in the bathroom and acted like I should be fine with it. What's your plan? What are you going to do with the mouse? How long do you plan to keep it in the bathroom?"

At this point, Beastie's survival seemed of such paramount importance to me that I completely missed what was making Casey so angry. In fact, it angered me that he couldn't see how important this was.

"Well, the only plan I really have is to try to keep it alive. It's not going very well. Couldn't you help me and root for its survival?" I asked.

Sadly, though I didn't see it, our marriage was dying. Casey was hurt that I was blatantly choosing to ignore his feelings and needs (something he felt I'd done time and again). Plus, any "normal" person would consider the consequences of deliberately bringing a wild mouse into their home and then handling it constantly. What kind of person was I that I didn't even have a plan? My behavior was showing him that I didn't consider him to be a priority in my life, that his opinion didn't count. I was thoughtless, controlling, and irresponsible.

From my perspective, however, there was no past where I'd ignored Casey's feelings and dictated what was happening. There was no future where I had worked out what to do with the mouse. There was only the present moment, and it didn't make sense to me why he would insist on tossing obstacles in my way when saving the mouse was hard enough as it was. Fundamentally, we had two very different goals: I had a mouse to save, right NOW; he had to plan his exit strategy from a woman who for some mystifying reason didn't seem to notice or care that her marriage was starving.

Neither of us, of course, had any idea of the ADHD symptoms at play in this scenario. Only looking back on it now do I see many of the hallmark traits of ADHD:

1. Impulsivity: I saw a compelling, immediate need, so I dropped everything in order to meet it. I mean, when a helpless baby mouse is right there at your feet, what're ya gonna do? Caught up in the moment, I made a split-second decision to apply my whole being to this new project. I certainly couldn't just ignore it in order to consider all of the pros and cons, make a detailed plan, or notify anyone else who also happened to live in the house.

2. Short-sightedness: I couldn't consider what would happen if a wild mouse escaped into the house, or if it had any diseases or ticks, or bit me, or what would happen to it once it was tame, or how my family would feel about it. Instead, I was sucked into the challenge of the moment. All that stuff about consequences and the future was just a vague blob with no temporal shape far out on the horizon somewhere. I'd deal with all that at some point that wasn't NOW.

3. The payoff of instant gratification: Unbeknownst to me, I was getting infusions of dopamine, one of the

neurotransmitters that's underactive in the ADHD brain, from each little thing I did to take care of the mouse. It was the high-stakes situation that helped give me that feel-good chemical and focus my attention.

4. Hyperfocus: My interest-based nervous system was, at that moment, interested in learning as much as I could about the baby mouse so that I could keep it alive. For the time being, little else existed for me outside of this intent.

5. Problems prioritizing: I picked out the details that seemed important, and I did them in an order that felt appropriate. The problem was that my brain wasn't giving me much help in terms of picking out the details that were the most important. For example, I prioritized feeding the mouse quickly over feeding the mouse appropriately. I also prioritized the mouse over my marriage because it seemed to me that the mouse needed me more.

6. Out of sight, out of mind: Casey was right, I hadn't considered his point of view because I'd actually forgotten all about him once the baby mouse had caught my attention. I only had room in my working memory for how to care for the mouse, so any potential notion of how Casey might feel when he returned from his trip disappeared into a black hole.

7. Emotional intensity: I was so caught up in my feelings of compassion for the mouse that I couldn't step back and look objectively at my behavior. I assumed that

Casey should feel the same emotional intensity about the mouse that I did.

Even as that mouse was dying, by golly I fed it. Even as my marriage was dying, by golly I was too busy creeping into the bathroom feeding a mouse baby formula to notice. I have a chronic problem with recognizing the imminent arrival of death, in fact. My sick guinea pigs, my hospitalized grandma, my poisoned rabbit, my heart-diseased dog drowning from her own fluid-filled lungs – How was I supposed to know where all that was heading? When Beastie died a few days later, I buried it in the backyard. It was the death of another one of my good intentions. I had kept trying to feed Beastie up until the moment the poor thing had expired. I misinterpreted or failed to notice all the signs leading to its demise. The tragedy was that I was just working with faulty tools, and if only I'd known it maybe I could have procured a different outcome – for both the mouse and my marriage.

3

Looking Where We're
Going and Remembering
Where We've Been

Even when I DO have a guide – my GPS, for example – telling me exactly what to pay attention to, I'm still a liability out on the road. Like so many other ADHD-ers, I'm absolutely hopeless with directions, and I'm not, surprise surprise, a great driver. I did finally learn basic traffic patterns, but I still managed to fail my driver's test the first time I took it. I remember driving my old Ford around the test course at age 16, the evaluator in my passenger seat marking things on his clipboard. I was being so careful to keep my speed steady and to stay on the right side of the road. I began braking well ahead of time at every STOP sign. I was almost at the end of the course, and as I drove over the crosswalk the evaluator said matter-of-factly

"Well, you just killed a pedestrian."

"Wait, what, but nobody was there!" I protested.

"You were supposed to act as if they were."

He told me I'd failed the test and would have to retake it. I had a hard time controlling my anger. He expected me to act as if this simulated neighborhood were a real neighborhood with other cars and pedestrians to contend with? How was I supposed to know that?! I'd been paying attention to demonstrating my skills, not to demonstrating my imagination.

If I could actually take a driver's test of my imagination, I'd pass it with flying colors! It's what my mind is constantly doing while I'm driving – keeping me engaged with daydreams and speculations and working over problems and solutions and feelings about things. That's why, even when I *know* how to get somewhere, there's about a 50% daily chance that I will be driving down the road in my own town and realize I don't know where I am. That goes up to 99% if I'm in an unfamiliar city. It happens like this: I'm driving along complacently, not even aware that my mind has drifted off. I randomly notice the old dog being walked (because he looks like he's laboring along, but awww he seems so happy to be out), the green of the moss on a lawn (I've always liked that color green. I'd like to paint a wall that color), and the next thing I know I look around me and think "Wait, where am I?!" I don't recognize any landmarks. I don't know if I've already taken that right turn I should have taken. I don't recall how long I've been in the car. I feel mildly panicked as I pull up to a STOP sign. I don't know which way to go.

As an example, last week I went to my yoga class like I usually do every Saturday. The studio is ten minutes from my house. Afterwards, I was supposed to pick up my partner's 16 year old daughter who lived in the neighborhood across the street from the one in which I was taking yoga. When yoga ended, I chatted with people, rolled up my mat, put my props away, and got in the car. I remembered that I was supposed to pick up Emma. I was proud of myself for remembering my obligation. I very intentionally began to drive, reminding myself all along that I needed to go to the other neighborhood. I got to the edge of the yoga neighborhood and looked around me. I didn't recognize anything. I tentatively made a right-hand turn and drove for a while hoping something would look familiar. It finally did. I ended up at Emma's high school, the very school I hadn't been able to find the week before when I'd offered to drop her off at an orchestra concert. I was nowhere near her house and I couldn't figure out what I'd done wrong. I literally could not find my way ACROSS THE STREET.

Between missing the obvious and honing in on the wrong details, I still get tripped up trying to follow my GPS. My GPS tells me "Take the next right," and I see two rights approaching. Is it actually the next right, the one that turns into that alley up there, or is it the next real right, the one that curves off onto that scary looking ramp? Or is it that partial right I just passed? And then, as some of my senses are hyper-attuned, god forbid my attention suddenly gets grabbed, not by the turn I was looking for but by that beautiful big bird I suddenly glimpse through my sunroof as I'm hurtling down the road.

The good news is that I'm totally fine with getting lost in a corn maze. In fact, every fall I seek out corn mazes just to have the satisfaction of taking part in an activity where everyone gets lost and it's all part of the process. Do I ever find the exit? Well, admittedly I've had to be airlifted out of some of the bigger corn mazes when my water and food ran out, but it's all part of the fun. Casey and I used to take our son, Leo, to corn mazes. After a while, Casey stopped joining us because he got irritated and panicky. When I asked what was wrong, he said he hated being lost and it felt terrible not knowing what direction in which to go. He was a man who needed to be in control at all times, and it was scary not to be in control. Poor guy, scared by a little corn maze. If he wandered my brain, he'd be terrified.

I used to refer to Casey as my external hard drive because he held the memories of our vacations, our family celebrations, and the everyday details of our life together in easily accessible file folders in his brain, organized by date and time, complete with thumbnail mental images. He remembered where we traveled, what we did, even the food we ate and how to get to our favorite places should we wish to return there.

Everyone notices particular details and creates deeper, long-term memories when specific emotions are attached to the information or experience, but the ADHD brain needs those emotions even more in order for details to register and memories to stick. What I register and record into memory from my life experiences are just snippets of things with no labels and in no particular order. I don't remember names of towns, things we did, or when we did them, ("Wait, where was that, again?"), but I can recall very specific moments barely situated in time and space: an artist at an open air market sleeping in the back of a truck with his paintings hanging on a wire nearby; a man on a wooden bridge making leather flip-flops decorated with elaborate leather flowers; fish from a street vendor eaten on a bench after a long walk. I couldn't tell you where each of these images came from, but I know I am able to hold onto them because of the emotions that accompany them.

I remember feeling confused and sorry for the artist sleeping so vulnerably in the back of his truck in the middle of the day while potential customers were browsing the market. The flip-flops I remember because I agonized over which pair to buy as a souvenir, and then later I felt guilty because, though they were beautiful, they were too uncomfortable to wear, and I got rid of them. The meal of fish I recall because it was surprisingly fresh and tasty and because as we sat on that bench somewhere in Greece (I think), Casey told me how much he enjoyed traveling with me. Since he was generally displeased by my performance in our marriage, it felt particularly good to hear him say that.

The other day, my son told me (from the back seat of the car) that it was tiring to take care of me. I asked him what he meant. He said "Well, you make the meals and stuff, but I always have to help you figure out directions and tell you where the house is and keep you from getting distracted and being late for things, and remind you what time it is and what you need to be doing. It's exhausting. You're a woman, you're supposed to be three times as able to multitask as a man. But you can't do it at all." It hurt me to realize that this is what he sees. All this stuff gets in the way and he can't appreciate the creative, loving, thoughtful mom that he has. I imagine my brain is a dense web of vines and thorns that extends for miles. The vines are so thick that you can't even see the castle they have enveloped, and you wouldn't even know that inside that castle is Sleeping Beauty, an incredibly smart, competent, efficient, highly talented, natural-born leader who is just taking a little lifelong nap.

4

Problems with Behavioral Inhibition

When my son was almost two years old, his first complete sentence was "How'd that happen?" It's pretty telling about the state of your household when your child suddenly takes notice and questions how it all got to this point.

Another way to phrase his question is "What was the cause of this effect?" The ability to connect cause to effect, to control one's actions in such a way as to elicit desired outcomes and to avoid undesirable ones, is not a strong suit of those of us with ADHD. Rather, we tend to get caught up in the "now" of our experiences and then find ourselves surprised when we discover rather abruptly where those experiences took us. We gather speed, can't stop to take stock objectively (where perhaps we might have fine-tuned our actions towards a particular outcome), and then continue on, often blindly out of control. Finally, something happens to change our course for us such as reaching an inevitable consequence. John K. Durall, a licensed marriage, family, and child counselor, explains the problem:

> *The ADHD person, in the presence of stimuli, is less able to stop or prevent an immediate, powerful, or automatic (helpful or harmful) response. This diminished behavioral inhibition then interacts with and leads to diminished functioning of the other brain operations dealing with self-regulation [non-verbal memory, verbal memory, self-talk, emotions, motivation, arousal states, problem analyzing, problem solving, and thought and behavioral sequencing].*

In other words, in the presence of stimuli, we are unable to direct our actions and recognize that "If I do (or don't do) this thing, this other thing will (or won't) happen." This is because we have difficulty inhibiting our automatic, unregulated behaviors, urges, and emotions. We jump in (or out) with both feet without stepping back first to determine if we should be resisting temptation, delaying gratification, or controlling our impulses because of social norms.

As a result of our powerful response to the stimuli, our brains literally dull our ability to engage in the self-regulatory executive functions that might steer us in a particular direction. Compared to our neurotypical peers, there is less of a gap between stimulus and response. Hence, we don't get the same opportunity to use past experiences to plan for future outcomes. Durall Concludes, "Therefore, the person's behavior often appears disorganized, irresponsible, chaotic, and ill directed."[14] Like Dorothy in "The Wizard of Oz," we might begin with a vague sense of dis-ease or a desire for something, and then suddenly we're riding through a tornado, crash-landing on a wicked witch, opening the door of our house to find a technicolor land of little people, and then wondering "Huh, how'd that happen?"

Let me tell you about my stalk of corn. Next to the steps leading up to my front door is some nice green ground cover, mostly pachysandra, wild strawberries, and weeds. One day, early in the summer, I noticed a stalk of green beginning to shoot up out of that ground cover. I almost pulled it, thinking it was a weed, but it looked so different from everything around it that I was curious what it would become. Over the weeks, it developed into a stalk of corn. It was so totally random and out of place by my front door that even the Amazon delivery person commented on it. He asked "How'd that happen?" I shrugged my shoulders and said I had no idea. The cause of that stalk of corn was a total mystery to me. Maybe a bird pooped and a seed sprouted? Maybe a squirrel did it? Heck, maybe I deliberately planted it and just didn't

---

[14] Durall, John K. Toward an Understanding of ADHD: A Developmental Delay in Self-Control. Camping Magazine, v72 n1 p38-41 Jan-Feb 1999. American Camp Association. www.acacamps.org. Accessed July 10, 2019.

remember doing it. There are so many things in my life that pop up as a direct result of my actions, yet they catch me utterly by surprise.

This can lead to some pretty humorous (or embarrassing) situations. For example, this past Sunday morning, I decided to weed my garden. I was out there for a couple of hours getting all hot and sweaty, and when I came inside I stripped off my clothes in the laundry room. One of my casual skirts was on the drying rack, so I put that on temporarily until I got upstairs to have a shower. However, there were no other shirts in the laundry room to put on, so I remained topless as I began washing my socks in the laundry sink.

My partner, Ben, was sewing in the other room, and he was dialed into our Zoom church service on his phone. I finished with my socks, hung them to dry, and then went into the sewing room to sit on a stool and listen to the minister for a few minutes before I went upstairs to take a shower. The sermon was really good, and I wanted to hear the rest of it, but I was hungry from weeding and I wanted to go upstairs to the kitchen in order to eat and to view the service on my computer screen. So, I went upstairs, retrieved my laptop, set it on the kitchen counter, and logged in to the service (all the while thinking about the leftover fried potatoes I was going to take out of the fridge). It wasn't until the video camera on my laptop suddenly revealed my topless self on the screen that I remembered I hadn't finished getting dressed! As I dove out of sight of the camera, I couldn't quite figure out how that had happened.

If we look at the situation through the lens of Mr. Durall's explanation, however, my behavior makes more sense. In the presence of stimuli (the sermon and the food in the fridge), I responded with interest and craving, respectively. This response was so all-encompassing that it diminished my self-regulating mechanisms (such as self-talk: "Hey, Vanessa, you're topless. Go put on some clothes before you end up on camera"). Most people would have been able to imagine their potential future embarrassment arising from this error in judgment, but I was stuck in the "now" of the immediate stimuli – the interesting sermon as well as my anticipation of those fried potatoes that I just needed to heat up. I was getting little hits of the feel-good chemical, dopamine, because my interest was piqued by the sermon and because I was anticipating eating those potatoes. In the wake of these compelling stimuli, how was I supposed to remember that I was half-naked?

Behavioral disinhibition frequently happens to women when they are giving birth. Social expectations such as refraining from cursing, remaining clothed, not impulsively yelling at others, or obeying a doctor's or midwife's directions often go out the window because the here and now of the body being overwhelmed by the experience of labor is more powerful and exerts more demands on the woman's attention than anything else. When her body is being hijacked by the processes of labor, a woman is a lot less likely to be able to inhibit urges, emotions, or impulses. Similarly, with ADHD, our brains are hijacked ALL THE TIME by powers that we cannot resist. We respond to the noise and intensity of certain stimuli far more than our neurotypical peers. And in those moments, our self-regulating executive functions are all but erased. We cannot apply the brakes. We are flotsam and jetsam floating in the river of time.

Living with unmanaged adult ADHD can be pretty funny, but it can also be devastating. It means living with chaos, anxiety, regret, and shame. It means beating yourself up all the time for not doing the things you meant or wanted to do. It means worrying that you're a bad parent who can't provide enough structure for your children. It means comparing yourself to others who seem to do so much more than you think you could ever do, and feeling stupid. It means high stress from desperately trying to keep up despite an invisible handicap and from pretending you know what you're supposed to be doing, even though you zoned out and didn't realize it. It means being terrified that you'll make the wrong decision, or mismanage your money, or forget the future exists, and end up living in a trash heap with rats for your friends. It is not a small thing. It affects most areas of your life.

A large number of people with ADHD get involved with high-risk behaviors and dependencies. For example, substance abuse (especially alcohol or cocaine), compulsive eating, compulsive shopping, caffeine and nicotine dependence, high-risk recreational activities, or other behavioral addictions such as pornography and sex-addiction. With our brains wired with the need for stimulation and problems with behavioral inhibition, we make impulsive decisions, don't adequately assess risks, and disregard social norms in the service of these stimuli. People with ADHD are particularly vulnerable to these addictive types of stimuli because they can provide us with a short-term clarity of focus and kick of motivation that eludes us. They make us feel momentarily in control. However, paradoxically, they also further blunt our ability to self-regulate and employ goal-directed behavior.

Research has shown that ADHD is associated with genes which govern cells that both receive and transmit dopamine to the brain. Dopamine is one of the chemicals in the brain called a neurotransmitter. These neurotransmitters help deliver messages from one nerve cell to another across the synapses (tiny spaces) between neurons. When the levels of dopamine are increased, the neurons needed for a task are put into action while the background "firing" of neurons that would normally lead to distraction is suppressed. This allows the brain to transmit a clearer signal. Dopamine functions as our natural reward system that helps us select the most important task and summon the motivation to do it, follow through on projects, and reinforces a job well done so that we will likely do it again in the future.

Another neurotransmitter that is affected with ADHD is serotonin. Serotonin affects our moods, our sleep, our social behavior, and our memory. With lower levels of serotonin, we exhibit more impulsive, defiant, frustrated, or impatient behavior. We are also more forgetful, as anyone who's ever experienced the "out of sight, out of mind" phenomenon well knows.

There are specific genes that are responsible for managing the expression of neurotransmitters, and research suggests that people with ADHD have rarer variants of these genes which cause some dysfunction in how the neurotransmitters operate. A variant in a particular dopamine receptor gene, for example, causes too few dopamine receptor sites to be available for using the amount of dopamine our brains produce. With decreased dopamine receptors to receive the feel-good chemical, we find it impossible to summon the motivation to do low-interest, mundane tasks, or to recognize the significance of particular tasks as opposed to others. Everything gets equal billing and grabs an equal amount of attention (or none at all).

A variation in the gene that encodes the dopamine transporter protein, on the other hand, can cause the brain to remove dopamine too quickly from receptor sites before it's had an opportunity to fully take effect. Dopamine transporters are proteins that move messages across the synapses between neurons. They are like boats carrying dopamine's specific messages to their destination (the specific neurons that act as dopamine receptors). The transporter releases the dopamine into the receptor in order for it to communicate its message, and once the message has been communicated, the transporter then re-absorbs the dopamine and carries it back (this keeps all of our emotions and other processes relatively steady). With this gene variant, the dopamine may not be given enough time to fully communicate its message before it's whisked away again, leaving the person with ADHD symptoms.

In the absence of enough available dopamine, in an effort to get our neurons firing to provide us with clarity and motivation, we engage in stimulation-seeking behaviors. Clinical Psychologist Dr. Ellen Littman explains:

> *Deficits in the reward pathway, including decreased availability of dopamine receptors, decrease motivation. Indeed, ADHD brains struggle to sustain motivation when rewards are mild or linked to long-term gratification. As a result, ADHD brains are constantly searching for stimulation that can increase dopamine quickly and intensely.*[15]

I remember my ex-husband working on an essay in graduate school. We were living together at the time, and I was trying to be a writer. I asked him how he was able to stay so focused, and he said "I love anticipating that stack of fresh white paper coming out of the printer when my essay is finished." He was capable of remaining focused on his work because of an anticipated payoff at some point in the future when the paper was done. The man could squeeze dopamine out of the thought of printer paper! Meanwhile, I was sitting at my desk with a box of Wheat Thins and a bag of carrots, chewing like a bunny, desperately trying to stimulate my brain's

---

[15] Littman, E. (2023, Oct. 23). © 1998 – 2023 WebMD LLC. All rights reserved. *Never Enough? Why ADHD Brains Crave Stimulation. ADDitudemag.com. https://www.additudemag.com/brain-stimulation-and-adhd-cravings-dependency-and-regulation/*

reward feedback loop in order to sustain my motivation to write.

One reason why stimulant medications, called "re-uptake inhibitors," lessen ADHD symptoms is because they keep the dopamine from being reabsorbed too quickly. By increasing the amount of dopamine available in the neural synapses, the stimulant medication makes dopamine-dependent neural signals more efficiently transmitted.[16] When the dopamine is available for use for a longer period of time, it can more fully express its message, and we can more fully experience the feeling of reward that helps us organize ourselves, motivate, and follow through with plans.[17] With our reward system boosted, we can be motivated by less immediate rewards and be able to control our behavior towards anticipated outcomes rather than towards immediate gratification.

Norepinephrine, a neurochemical synthesized by the body from dopamine that acts as both a stress hormone and as a neurotransmitter, is also affected in its expression by certain gene variants. Norepinephrine is part of the adrenal system and acts on various neuronal receptors to help us stay alert, increasing blood pressure, the amount of blood flowing to the heart, and blood sugar levels to provide more energy to the body. Low levels of norepinephrine are responsible for our

---

[16] Roberts, Kevin. Movers Dreamers and Risk-Takers: Unlocking the Power of ADHD. Hazelden, 2012. 203-204.

[17] Margaret Austin, PhD. *Gulfbend.org*. n.d. 22 April 2021.
<https://www.gulfbend.org/poc/view_doc.php?type=doc&id=13861>.

lack of alertness and wakefulness in activities that aren't highly stimulating. Low levels also cause problems with long term memory storage. High levels, on the other hand, can worsen anxiety and hyperactivity.[18] Finally, too much dopamine in the wrong places can also cause symptoms of hyperactivity and impatience.

Suffice it to say, people with ADHD suffer impairments in the regulation of the brain's dopamine and adrenal systems. Certain gene variants that code for neurochemical pathways seem to be responsible for this regulatory impairment in folks with ADHD. "These altered pathways seem to lead to dysfunctions in executive functions, alertness, learning, and motivation, among other difficulties."[19] Depending on which gene variants we have, we may present with more of certain symptoms than others. For example, some of us may have more issues with poor judgment, restlessness, and self-control, while others of us may struggle most mightily with forgetfulness and poor organization.

In addition, studies utilizing functional magnetic resonance imaging also reveal structural differences in our brains. We have reduced gray matter and decreased cortical thickness in certain areas, especially around the right prefrontal cortex. Interestingly, there is also some indication that the

---

[18] Bancos, I. (Ed.). (2022, January 24). Copyright © 2023 Endocrine Society. All rights reserved. Adrenal Hormones. Endocrine.org. https://www.endocrine.org/patient-engagement/endocrine-library/hormones-and-endocrine-function/adrenal-hormones/

[19] Roberts, Kevin. Movers Dreamers and Risk-Takers: Unlocking the Power of ADHD. Hazelden, 2012. 206.

structural differences in our ADHD brains are not consistent across genders. In one study, for example, boys with ADHD had significantly smaller basal ganglia volumes and significant differences in basal ganglia shapes as compared to their typically developing peers. Girls, on the other hand, did not show significant differences in the basal ganglia.[20]

A recent study co-authored by Dr. Russell Barkley, Savior of the Scattered, and Mariellen Fischer[21] examines the preponderance of self-destructive habits and lack of conscientiousness of people with ADHD and the effect of these things on life expectancy. They found that people with ADHD have more alcohol, tobacco, and drug use, and more difficulties quitting. They are three times as likely to be obese and to suffer from poor health (including type 2 diabetes) due to excessive carboydrate and sugar intake and binge or impulsive eating.

In addition, adults with ADHD "...are more than four times as likely to die of accidental injury [especially traumatic brain injury] by age 40." There is also a slightly increased suicide risk that factors into that statistic. This is how ADHD can shave off 9-13 years from someone's life. In a webinar following from the study, Dr. Barkley explains that "ADHD is markedly worse in its effects on life expectancy than all of the major risks that we're concerned about: diabetes, coronary

---

[20] Ibid 207

[21]Barkley, Russell, and Mariellen Fischer. "Hyperactive Child Syndrome and Estimated Life Expectancy at Young Adult Follow-Up: The Role of ADHD Persistence and Other Potential Predictors." *Sage Journals*, Journal of Attention Disorders , https://journals.sagepub.com/. 2019 Jul;23(9):907-923. doi: 10.1177/1087054718816164. Epub 2018 Dec 10.

heart disease, smoking, alcohol, obesity, nutrition, and so on. Indeed, you could combine the top four risk factors in the population for early death, and ADHD exceeds that combination of those four risk factors."[22]

My own experience with self-destructive behavior began midway through college. As academic pressures continued to increase, I developed an eating disorder. It was the 1990's, and the "low fat" craze of the time gave me something tangible that I could completely control, in contrast to the many essays I had to write where I had to wrestle my messy and disorganized thinking into some sort of brilliant research, analysis, and thesis. The only way for me to write a paper, or to do other low-stimulation activities, was if I had a bottomless bag or box of food (usually wheat thins and baby carrots, or boxes of low-fat chocolate cookies) always within reach.

I also binge-ate chocolate chips, bowls of blueberries, and any other small finger foods that I could fairly continuously pop in my mouth with one hand in-between typing. (That's probably why, over time, I ended up with a keyboard that resembled panko-encrusted chicken tenders). I needed the constant sensory stimulation in order to keep my neurons firing and my ideas flowing. If I didn't have food nearby, my brain shut down and I fell asleep. (This was especially dangerous when I was driving, but I'll get to that in a minute). This habit of binging sugar and carbohydrates was a

---

[22] Barkley, Russell. © 1998-2023 WebMD, LLC. All rights reserved How ADHD Shortens Life Expectancy. What Parents and Doctors Need to Know to Take Action. Webinar. Additudemag.com. January 29, 2019.

work-around for a problem I didn't know I had. Dr. Ellen Littman explains:

> *ADHD brains exhibit decreased glucose metabolism compared to non-ADHD brains, resulting in less energy available to the attention center in the prefrontal cortex. As a result, ADHD brains send out distress messages demanding more glucose, and the owners of those brains suddenly crave sugary foods and carbohydrates, which can be quickly converted into glucose. Glucose increases dopamine and serotonin, so brains experience pleasure and greater calm.*[23]

I didn't know that my developmentally delayed brain needed extra stimulation in order not to shut down on these tasks that held low interest for me, and that this wasn't a typical experience for everyone. We all do the best we can with what we have to work with, and self medicating with food is a common symptom of people with ADHD precisely because it improves our attention and calms us down.

It can take a long time for us to realize when our behaviors don't line up with the majority of people's, and to figure out why we are drawn to activities that are self destructive or risky. We aren't trying to be self destructive, we're just trying to find balance. Unfortunately, "As a result of

[23] Littman, Ellen PhD. (2023, October 23). Copyright © 1998 - 2023 WebMD LLC. All rights reserved. Never Enough? Why ADHD Brains Crave Stimulation. Additudemag.com. https://www.additudemag.com/brain-stimulation-and-adhd-cravings-dependency-and-regulation

these self-regulation problems, ADHD is predisposing people to all kinds of adverse outcomes – in education, family functioning, peer relationships… difficulties with driving, antisocial behavior, risky sexual behavior, occupational function."[24]

It's kind of like being a frog. Amphibians are dependent on external cues and environmental conditions for temperature regulation and hence for their very survival. If a frog suns itself on a rock for too long, it will dry out and die. But if it stays in cold water for too long, it will freeze to death or get a fungal infection. Our ADHD brains are also dependent on external cues and our environment for self-regulation. We need alarms, visual reminders, and immediate rewards or dire consequences to get us to shift appropriately from sunny rock to cold water and back again.

Frogs, however, have a better sense of the consequences of their actions than we do. Left entirely to our own devices, without the proper environmental support, many of us begin to self-destruct. We stay in that nice cool water until we're too cold to get out. We seek out those "feel-good" experiences in the now, and we don't give much thought to the "not now" until we feel SO BAD. Even though we may repeat this process over and over again, we don't really learn from the consequences. In fact, when it all catches up with us, we're rather surprised. This dialogue between a neurotypical frog (Frog B) and a frog with ADHD (Frog A) illustrates my point:

---

[24] Barkley, Russell. Copyright © 1998 - 2023 WebMD LLC. All rights reserved. "How ADHD Shortens Life Expectancy. What Parents and Doctors Need to Know to Take Action." Webinar. Additudemag.com. January 29, 2019.

Frog B: I just love this swamp. That was really fun swimming around with you.

Frog A: Yeah, this is so great. Let's play hide and seek in the water.

Frog B: I think I might be feeling a little cold, so I'm gonna climb out on that rock and sit in the sun for awhile

Frog A: Really? But we haven't even explored that log down there, and I want to swim some races and see if I can beat my best time, and it's just so exhilarating to dive and swim.

Frog B: Yes, but you're going to get too cold and it's not going to be fun anymore. You should get out. Come on, and join me on this rock.

Frog A: Yeah, yeah, but I'm not cold NOW. Watch how fast I can go!

Frog B: This rock is nice and warm. You should try it.

Frog A: I bet I can reach the bottom and come back up in five seconds.

Frog B: You might not come back up. You're too cold. You need to get out.

Frog A: Ready? Here I go – 1…2…3!

Frog B: Frog A? Frog A? Where are you?

Frog A: (pops up, shivering) Oh man, I feel horrible. Help me out. I was having so much fun a second ago. I don't get it. Now I feel like I'm gonna pass out. How'd that happen?

When we can't inhibit our behavior adequately, we end up like Frog A, in over our heads and unable to get out on our own. Not being able to inhibit our behavior appropriately causes us to be at the mercy of external stimuli. We live our lives alternating between these three modes: stimulation-seeking, stimulation-avoiding, and stimulation swept-away. Each of these modes is fraught with peril.

In stimulation-seeking mode, we can get into trouble with addictions; in stimulation-avoiding mode, we can get into trouble with becoming overwhelmed and behaving inappropriately as a result; in stimulation swept-away mode, we can get so caught up in something that we hyperfocus on it to the complete disregard of everything else (responsibilities, family, the need to get dressed, etc). A particular doozy is when our brains are in two of these modes at once, as in my next example.

Last week, I was headed home from a friend's house an hour away. It was dusk, and a storm was just starting to roll in. I was shaky on the directions out of her city back to the highway, and, as usual, (despite the GPS) I made a few wrong turns. As I tried intently to make sense of what Gloria (my GPS lady) was telling me to do, and streets kept veering off in two different directions, the sky opened up and it began to pour. Because there were so many turns and decisions, I was able to stay focused, but once I found the highway home, I started to drift. Cars were literally drifting off the road due to hydroplaning (in fact, I passed four accidents), but I was drifting in my head: the lightning was making magnificent designs in the sky ahead of me, the thunder was SO LOUD, there were people without their lights on, tractor trailers were in the passing lane, and I was feeling lulled by it all. My senses were so overwhelmed that they began to dull. I drove straight ahead on cruise control, and I became less and less alert. Once the panic of being lost had passed, all the sensory stimulation had an overwhelming "shutting down" effect on my brain (aka stimulation-avoiding).

My brain wanted to shut down to protect itself from all the input, but I knew if I let that happen, I'd have an accident. Paradoxically, I needed to override the stimulation-avoiding by stimulation-seeking. I needed some sensory input over which I had more direct control. It was then that I remembered my pistachio nuts. In my backpack on the passenger seat, I had a bag of roasted, salted pistachio nuts in their shells. Steering with my left hand, I reached into the bag and felt around for the pistachios. I pulled it out, brought it to my lap, and began cracking shells and popping pistachios with a fervor only a fellow ADHD-er desperate to command some focus would know.

Yes, of course shelling pistachio nuts while driving in a blinding rain in the dark was dangerous, but it was a lot less dangerous than the alternative – falling asleep at the wheel and becoming one of those accidents I witnessed as I drove. Careening through space at 70MPH in the dark storm, my brain and I were embroiled in an intense battle. Every time it tried to shut off to avoid the overwhelming stimulation of the storm (THUNDER ROLL, BOOM, HAMMERING RAIN), I poked at it with a pistachio nut (CRACK, CLICK,

CRUNCH) to get it to wake up and remain alert (stimulation-seeking). It was an onomatopoeic battle of epic proportions!

Because our lack of dopamine means we ADHD-ers can't necessarily access the appropriate neurons for the task at hand, the background noise of many neurons responding to sensory input sometimes becomes too intense. Some ADHD brains are so overwhelmed by a bombardment of reactions to sensory input that we struggle to reduce the excessive stimulation by tuning out, avoiding group activities and overwhelming tasks, and isolating ourselves. (Or we may simply "shut down" and fall asleep). We may exhibit high anxiety as a result of all this overstimulation, and these escape behaviors are our coping mechanism. Whether it's in summoning motivation or becoming overwhelmed too quickly, the ADHD brain is either under-stimulated or over-stimulated, but the unique balance of stimulation that enables optimal functioning eludes us.

If you just don't know when to quit, or how to quit, or even that you ought to quit, or if you're often on a path towards some catastrophe or another but only notice it and take any action to avoid it when it smacks you in the face, I extend to you my invitation to the "How'd *that* happen?" club. And, I also encourage you to seek help in managing your ADHD if you haven't already, before this becomes your real epitaph.

5

Blaming Others for Our Outcomes

The following event, that occurred in 2002 before my ADHD diagnosis, is a perfect example of how we ADHD-ers move between extremes and can't seem to find a middle-ground (unless you call "middle-ground" the middle of the road on the side of a volcano, but we'll get to that). Because I didn't know for so long that my brain was wired for ADHD, I had no explanation when I did something wrong or forgot something or missed an important detail. To deflect blame and the feeling of failure that came with it, I had a tendency to blame others for the things that happened to me.

Most of us do this to some extent. Taking personal responsibility is hard. But for me, it felt like there was always a missing piece to the puzzle, and someone else was deliberately keeping that piece from me. If only they had been clearer or provided me with the crucial information that I needed, we could have avoided a lot of suffering and misunderstanding.

While everyone else was stepping lightly over piles of manure, I was blundering right into them. Why couldn't they just point out the pitfalls? I frequently got to the effect of my actions, realized I had achieved an unpleasant result, and then found out that everyone else knew something I didn't that allowed them to circumvent the problem. Along with "How was I supposed to know?" a similar refrain was "Why didn't you tell me that before?" whenever things got messy for me. Yes, I blamed my friends and family. They were supposed to be looking out for me. They were supposed to share their knowledge. Their response was always "I thought you knew." Sadly, I didn't know. I was blind to the obvious, to the future, to cause and effect, to others' reactions. I was swinging between extremes with my inability to self-regulate, desperately trying to hold it all together. This inability to self-regulate is how I almost ended up as roadkill on a volcano in Maui.

The Maui Sunrise Volcano Bike Tour

Upon arrival at the 10,023 foot summit you will be escorted by your guides to the rim of the crater where you will view the spectacular sunrise.

Your tour then proceeds to the 6,500 foot level of Haleakala where you will receive a comprehensive safety briefing and begin your 26-mile bike ride down the slopes of Haleakala – the world's largest dormant volcano.

(I wish they'd added a disclaimer to this lovely description: DO NOT ATTEMPT IF YOU HAVE UNDIAGNOSED AND UNMANAGED ADHD!)

The sunrise at the top was beautiful. Haleakala means "house of the sun" in Hawaiian, and indeed it seemed like the sun was so close as its beams climbed up onto the clouds around us. The sky became saturated with oranges, reds, and yellows as particles of sun slowly emerged. The sunrise revealed an almost Martian landscape with red-streaked, cratered lava vents surrounding the summit, jagged cinder cones all pointing up the slope like rows of sharks' teeth, and volcanic rock rubble strewn about. A hearty but endangered plant called the ahinahina (silversword) squatted firmly here and there among the rocks. These plants can live for up to a century, but they flower only once. Once they flower they die, their seeds scattering from tall flower stalks.

Scottie, our guide, took a picture of my husband and me perched on a clump of cinder cones with the lip of the "house of the sun's" crater behind us. We had chosen a tour company that would set us up with all our gear and a safety briefing and then let us navigate down the volcano at our own pace. Scottie handed us our windbreaker jumpsuits, special all-weather jackets, large padded gloves, and full-face motorcycle helmets. I remember thinking all the gear seemed a bit much. Then Scottie told us to remember one crucial thing: Don't squeeze the brakes too hard, or you'll find that your bike has stopped and you're still going – right over the handlebars. "It happens," he said. "People get up a bunch of speed, and then they panic and hit the brakes. Just keep a gentle pressure on the brakes the whole time, and don't let yourself get out of control."

Thinking back on this now, I'm reminded of the Greek myth of Icarus and Daedelus. Attempting to escape from the tower where they were imprisoned, Daedalus fashioned for himself and his son two pairs of gigantic wings made out of feathers and wax. He warned his son to keep to the middle, following his father's careful path between the sky and the sea. For if Icarus flew too close to the sun, the heat would melt the wax on the wings and he would fall. If he flew too close to the sea, the dampness would weigh down the wings and he would be dragged into the sea and drown. But Icarus couldn't self-regulate. The euphoria of flight was too much for him, and he soared up and up into the sky. He swooped high up and far down, high up and far down, until inevitably he came too close to the sun, and the wax holding the feathers in place melted. Poor Icarus kept flapping and flapping his featherless arms to no avail as he plummeted into the sea below and drowned.

The people in our tour group began their descent, a few at a time, and Scottie got back into his 15 person van and headed back down the volcano to his workplace. I was dilly-dallying looking for the perfect volcanic rock to bring home as a souvenir. When I found the right one – gray-black, oval, and covered in a shiny network of little holes – I put it into my backpack and Casey and I got on our bikes. We were the last of our group to begin our descent.

Casey let me go first to set the pace. [Note to User: NEVER LET SOMEONE WITH UNMANAGED ADHD SET THE PACE DOWN A VOLCANO]. At first it was delightful. The road was steep but smooth. There was a steady stream of cyclists whizzing past, as well as cars, vans, and buses headed back down from sunrise excursions. There were flower stands alongside the road at intervals that sold flowers the likes of which I'd never seen before. I glimpsed large, showy, pink flowers, and a majestic view beyond the guard rail in layers of blue, white, green, and brown as clouds hovered over the valley below us.

Our bikes quickly picked up speed, and I didn't quite know what to focus on. Should I go super fast and enjoy the rush of adrenaline? Should I slow down and check out the colorful flower stands? Should I take in every last drop of the view or keep my eyes peeled for tropical birds? In typical ADHD fashion, I tried to do all those things simultaneously. Like Icarus in the Greek myth, I sought more and more sensory stimulation until suddenly I was on stimulation overload, and I couldn't regulate my reactions. As I squeezed and let out the brakes erratically, in my mind it went something like this: "Wind in hair, so fast. Ooo, pretty flowers. Can't see, too fast. Ooo, I've never gone this fast. Ooo, more pretty flowers. I should look at those. Ooo, fast, stick with it. Enjoy the thrill of speed. Look how high up I am. Wow, what would happen if I flew off the side? No, slow, see flowers, enjoy the journey. Ooo, another flower stand. Darn, missed it. Fast, enjoy. No, slow, take it all in. No, fast, let it wash over me. No, slow"… BLACKOUT.

When I opened my eyes, I found myself face down, like a tackled football player, in the middle of a busy road on the side of a volcano. I had "flown too close to the sun," over the handlebars, and was now about 15 feet in front of my bicycle. My husband pulled up behind me and yelled at me to get out of the road. My body was going into shock and I couldn't make it get up, so Casey threw his bike aside, ran up to me, and hauled me to the side of the road. I lay there, badly scraped and bleeding, with groups of bike tours whizzing by and Casey telling me not to go to sleep. I wondered why none of the other bike tours were stopping to see if I was OK. Probably it was because they weren't fools. They all knew they couldn't stop that quickly.

After some assessment, we determined I hadn't broken anything. I was just badly bruised. And, thanks to the motorcycle helmet, my head and mouth seemed to be OK despite the impact with the ground. By then I was able to stand up, but I was too shaky and terrified to get back on the bike. Thankfully, a nice man who was driving by pulled over, offering to throw our bikes in the back of his pick-up and take us to his house where I could clean up. We gratefully got into his truck. What I remember most about the aftermath was standing at this stranger's kitchen sink washing the gravel and blood from my wounds with a lovely white embroidered hand towel and thinking "Why didn't he give me an old rag to use, instead?"

When I was done cleaning up, the man drove us all the way down Haleakala volcano to the bike shop where I told my story. We didn't see Scottie, but another tour guide asked if I had taken any volcanic rock from the top. I showed him the rock in my bag. That was when I found out that A) It's illegal to remove anything from Haleakala National Park and B) According to the indigenous religion of the Native Hawaiians, Pele, the goddess of the volcanoes, known for her fiery temper, curses people for taking a piece of her body (lava rock) away from her island home. There have been so many stories, in fact, of people having a string of bad luck after they've taken lava rocks home with them that thousands of pounds of lava rocks are shipped back to the islands of Hawaii each year.[25]

The tour guide was certain that it was my illegal rock that had been the cause of my bike accident. Pele was trying to stop me from leaving. I certainly didn't need a volcano goddess after me, so I left the rock with him to return to its sacred place atop the mountain, afraid Pele would curse all the people on the airplane if I attempted to take my souvenir home. I was pretty angry, though, that I hadn't been warned earlier. I said to the tour guide "Why didn't you tell me that before?!" I was certain it would have saved me a lot of pain and suffering to have known that a vengeful goddess rules the volcano and is very protective of her space.

I regretted that I never got to examine the pretty flowers and that I had only completed a small fraction of the bike ride down the volcano. I also regretted being so badly bruised that I could barely move the next day and being afraid for years to get on a bike at all. Plus, I kind of ruined Casey's

---

[25] https://www.wanderwisdom.com/travel-destinations/How-to-Return-Lava-Rocks-to-Hawaii

experience. But I was blaming the wrong person. It would have saved me many years of pain and suffering in my adult life and in my marriage if somebody *had told me before* that I had ADHD and showed me how it was hijacking my life.

6

Excuses, Excuses and Emotional Reactivity

My need to pin the blame for my shortcomings on someone or something else was a coping mechanism to stave off rejection and disapproval. How could something be my fault when I had tried my hardest with the resources available to me? "It's not *my* fault I was late. The phone rang and I had to talk to my mother." Or "It's not *my* fault the wash smells moldy. I couldn't take it out of the washer for a few hours because I was running errands." It hurt so badly when Casey got mad at me for messing something up or for not getting to something I had promised to do. I had physical symptoms related to feeling attacked: shallow breathing, racing heart, ice cold extremities. I would do anything to make that pain go away. I came up with excuses, I apologized, I redoubled my efforts to make Casey happy.

After Casey and I separated, and I finally got diagnosed with ADHD, I bought the book "*Is it You, Me, or Adult ADHD?*" by Gina Pera. I took a close hard look at some of the things Casey had accused me of in the past: not seeming to care about his needs because I always forgot what he asked for, not following through on commitments, being late all the time which showed lack of consideration for him, not doing my fair share of household chores, needing to control things because of my high anxiety, not having enough goals in life, blaming him for my mistakes. He had painted a picture of me as undependable, untrustworthy, uncaring, and unambitious. When I looked at all these things through the lens of an ADHD diagnosis, it was like in the original Superman where Superman turns back the entire planet and does a total reset. What if this whole wreckage of a marriage really *wasn't* my fault? What if together, with the help of this diagnosis, we turned back the planet and re-examined all of our old hurts and frustrations with an understanding of their cause?

The more research I did, the more hopeful I became that now we would finally have some explanations and resources to begin to heal our problems. I took the book to my estranged husband at his apartment and asked him to read it. I explained the diagnosis and how I thought my ADHD had greatly contributed to our issues. Casey said he would read the book, but he also made it clear that he was dubious and that I would have to work hard to prove to him that I could change. Considering how frustrated he had been over the 16 years of our marriage, this was probably a reasonable thing for him to say. But what I heard was that same old parent-child power dynamic that ADHD had helped set up long ago, where he was the competent one who took care of everything, and I had to prove I could handle responsibility. I was tired of having to prove my worth. I was tired of not being appreciated or recognized for my efforts while I struggled with being disabled by a world that was obviously rigged to favor the neurotypical.

After our conversation, he gave me a hug and said he appreciated that I'd talked to him about this. There was a sliver of possibility at that point that maybe he would read and understand. In my ideal world, he would come back to me and say "I get it now. You were working as hard as you could. You didn't want to disappoint me or yourself. You couldn't help it. It wasn't your fault. I can see that you have amazing creativity and strengths in areas where I'm weak. How can we work together to help you manage your ADHD and get the most out of your life and our lives together?" Yet when I left his apartment that day, it was pretty clear to me that wasn't going to happen.

He was going to wait, as he always did, for me to "fix" this thing on my own, with no attempt to examine how his own actions and expectations had contributed to our problems and my negative self-image. He was blameless, and I was the problem. That wasn't how I wanted to start the process of getting my ADHD under control. I needed him to truly support me, not to fold his arms and tap his foot waiting for me to get it right for once. I couldn't handle that cycle where I failed, felt rejected, and tried to pacify him anymore. I wasn't going back to that. That was when I squeezed the brakes, hard: Brakes, handlebars, blackout.

I awoke alone on an empty road, (metaphorically speaking). As much as I knew intellectually that my ADHD symptoms weren't my fault, Casey's rejection of me and of my contributions to our life together was agonizing.

Something I didn't know at the time was that an overwhelming percentage of people with ADHD have what is known as "Rejection Sensitive Dysphoria." It is yet another problem with self-regulation, this time involving the regulation of emotions:

> *RSD is an intense emotional response caused by the perception that you have disappointed others in your life and that, because of that disappointment, they have withdrawn their love, approval, or respect. The same painful reaction can occur when you fail or fall short of your rather high goals and expectations.*[26]

People who have RSD experience it as an almost unbearable pain when we experience rejection from others. Disapproval literally hurts us much more than it hurts neurotypical people. The thing is, our perception of rejection or dislike may not

---

[26] Broadbent , Elizabeth. (2019, October 10) ©1998-2023 WebMD LLC. All rights reserved. "ADHD, Women, and the Danger of Emotional Withdrawal." *ADDitudemag.com*, 3 Mar. 2022. www.additudemag.com/adhd-emotional-withdrawal-rejection-sensitivity-women/

even be accurate. Our senses are so hyper-attuned for attack that we may misinterpret a comment or a situation as criticism when there is none. Regardless, we cope by internalizing this perceived or real rejection, becoming depressed and losing self-esteem. We may try so hard to avoid the emotional pain of rejection that we become "people pleasers" in order to get others to approve of us, losing track of our own desires in the process. Conversely, we may externalize the pain and lash out in anger, verbally or physically. We may become bullies or have run-ins with the law, unable to manage our hurt and anger. We might also be afraid to try things in life unless we are sure we can immediately succeed.

While it is not thought at this point that RSD is caused by the experience of past trauma, it seems to me that past traumatic experiences probably make our emotional reactivity that much worse in adulthood. Peer rejection, bullying, people's reactions to our childhood impulsive outbursts, our daydreaming, or our dropping the ball teach us to anticipate criticism and put us on the defensive.

When I was young and I had committed some sort of infraction, my mother punished me by giving me the silent treatment to teach me a lesson. The pain of rejection was indescribable. I remember following my mom around the kitchen pleading with her to look at me: "Mommy PLEASE," I begged. "Mommy, it's not my fault." It seemed like her withdrawal of love lasted forever. After trying for some time to get her attention, I'd dejectedly return to my room, my brain churning with ideas for how to get her to love me again. One particular time I remember getting out a little heart-shaped plastic box of heart-shaped colored paper. On a purple heart, I wrote this note to my mom: "Mommy, please don't be mad at me. I love you."

Thinking back on that simple note now, I see myself asking some deep questions: Isn't love enough? What more could you possibly want from me than that? I love you, so why won't you love me back? Is anger really stronger than love? My mom kept that note tucked into the side of her mirror on her dresser for years and years. I like to think it reminded her of what was really important.

Perhaps my experience of abandonment was particularly brutal because of my ADHD-induced Rejection Sensitive Dysphoria, or perhaps that experience made me more naturally reactive to perceived rejection. I'll never know. I just know that I carried this intense emotional pain into adulthood whenever I was triggered by the same sort of withdrawal of approval or love. And I know that as much as divorce hurt, it didn't hurt as badly as the daily wounds of rejection I endured from my husband as I constantly disappointed him.

There are other areas as well where those of us with ADHD may experience difficulties with emotional regulation. If you've ever been waiting in line for too long and suddenly felt like you were going to blow a gasket, or people were crowding too close to you on the subway and you felt the intense desire to elbow all of them in the ribs, or you were three hours into listening to a time-share presentation and out of the blue you suddenly burst out with "This needs to END. RIGHT NOW!" or you were on the phone with a customer service representative who wasn't being helpful and you started cursing at them, you know what I'm talking about.

Most of us don't have much tolerance for criticism, rejection, waiting, or frustration. Nor do we have as much control as we would like over our reactions to these things. In addition, for many of us, our reactions are generally impulsive and we don't see them coming. I think, quite frankly, that we have a lot in common with Pele, the goddess of volcanoes. We can simmer with irritation for a certain amount of time and then explode in a dramatic spectacle, or we can grow cold and hard and withdraw emotionally into our lava cone. I feel sorry for the person who tries to take a piece of us home with no knowledge of our volatility.

7

Anxiety, Negativity, and Inflexibility

Grandma Toby was afraid. But we didn't know. When my sister and I were young, we just thought she was silly. We rolled our eyes and played along. Grandma Toby never seemed to go out or to do anything. My grandfather named his sailboat the "Minus-Toby" because Toby was too scared of water to go anywhere near it. She felt most safe and secure shuffling around in my their narrow kitchen, moving papers from one pile to another and eating stale cookies. In the kitchen, there was a black and white TV with a dusty pile of magazines on top. There was always an old movie or an Archie Bunker show on to keep Grandma Toby company.

Most of the rooms in my grandparents' house seemed to have been forgotten about and were exactly as they had been when my mom and her siblings were growing up there. When my sister and I were young and stayed with our grandparents for the weekend, Grandma Toby was afraid we'd fall, afraid we'd get hurt, afraid we'd wander too far away, afraid we'd choke, afraid we wouldn't put the clothes back on the dolls, afraid to open the curtains because "the sun will fade the furniture." So my sister and I played in the dark, in the back room with the blood red, shag carpet where no one but us ever went, and we swung around the heavy metal mace we found in the back closet and the sword we found under the couch.

Anxiety can be pretty paralyzing sometimes, and those of us with ADHD nervous systems have a high rate of co-existing anxiety. Like my grandmother, we are far better at imagining hideous and dire outcomes to events in our lives than we are at arranging our behavior to work towards desired effects (or at least to avoid unpleasant consequences) in reality. As my ex-husband pointed out in the corn maze, it is scary not to feel in control. No wonder that people with ADHD have much higher rates of anxiety. During the day, with my disorganized and stressful life, I'm chronically worried about forgetting to pay the bills, running out of gas, not getting my work done on time, being late to a meeting, or forgetting about the dog and leaving him in a hot car (guilty).

For me, I think that in order to cope with the places I've resigned myself to being pretty hopeless (navigation, math, paperwork, organization), I need to exercise twice as much control over the other stuff. I make rules for how things should be and I expect my family to follow them. In my mind,

I have very good reasons for these rules that involve cause and effect (the effect being an imagined terrible consequence that fuels my anxiety rather than an actual outcome for which there has been a precedent established). And because my brain isn't particularly able to sort out the big, important stuff from the small, inconsequential stuff, I'm relentless about my household following ALL the rules. I can't let things go.

For example, I used to insist on having separate cutting boards for garlic/onions vs. everything else. When I saw my ex-husband using the wrong cutting board, I knew that pineapple would taste like garlic and be RUINED. RUINED, I tell you! I had to speak up. It was a matter of great importance and urgency in that moment. When he took the trash out by just carrying the bag across the carpet to the front door, I just KNEW the bag was going to leak and leave a big, smelly spot on the rug. If he kept the bag in the plastic trash can until he got outside, he would avoid that terrible mistake. I had to tell him. When he left the compost bin on the floor without the lid, I knew it would be awful if our dog ate it and it killed the dog. So many things could lead to something terrible, awful, and horrible. We all had to be vigilant. (And of course, I was hyper-vigilant anyway thanks to my Rejection Sensitive Dysphoria. My senses were always on high-alert mode). You can imagine how this drove my ex-husband crazy. He told me to stop criticizing him, and believe me I tried. But my brain was wired on a one-way path to anxiety-ville.

My Grandpa Al was the exact opposite of my grandmother. He had built a successful small business for himself as a sign painter. In many ways, he was fearless. We have an old picture of him standing on top of a water tower that he'd finished lettering. He was very smart, yet he'd dropped out of school in the 7th grade. He taught himself photography, sailing, oil painting, and Spanish, to name just a few of his creative pursuits. He was restless, bull-headed, quick to anger, insatiably curious about the world, and impossible to please. He wouldn't listen to anyone when it came to making house and boat repairs or storing dangerous flammable materials in the basement. He did every small and large repair and building project himself because he refused to pay a professional, and it caused a lot of leaks and other damage that didn't need to happen.

My grandparents are an excellent illustration of how differently ADHD can manifest in different people. Neither of them was ever diagnosed with ADHD, but we know it runs in families, and based on their personality traits I wouldn't be at all surprised. Despite the fact that on the surface they seemed nothing alike – he was hyperactive and restless, always searching for high-stimulation activities; she was paralyzed by inertia – they both had a tendency towards extremes, an inability to self-regulate. She couldn't get herself moving; he couldn't stop doing things even when people tried to tell him it wasn't working. Both had a hard time following through on tasks. She couldn't put away the laundry always piled on the bed or throw out rotten food in the fridge; he couldn't seem to finish fixing the porch or mowing the lawn.

Many people with ADHD have the problematic tendency of being rigid, inflexible, and unable to compromise easily. My Grandpa Al's bull-headedness when it came to how he took care of his house is a good example. Rigidity is, in fact, a common ADHD trait because it interplays so much with our anxiety and a deficit in the executive function called cognitive flexibility (otherwise known as set or task-shifting). Like a dog with a bone, we grab hold of an idea/desire/way of doing something, and we can't seem to let it go.

The dogged pursuit of a task or an idea, even when it's not working out, even when we know we need different tools for the job or we should have done something differently, is called "perseveration." Essentially, it's persevering to the extreme with a process or idea even when it is no longer adequate or functional. I used to think I was just a perfectionist, but it's so much more complicated than that. Imagine all of our unregulated impulses as a train. Sometimes it's going super fast, smashing into anything that unwittingly tries to cross the tracks; sometimes it can't get moving at all. And sometimes it needs to switch tracks (i.e. take a different approach) to get to the destination.

Problems with behavioral inhibition mean that those of us with ADHD are not in control of our railroad switches (those crucial places where the tracks veer off in different directions). Our switchman, who should live in our prefrontal cortex and help us task switch when necessary, is only about eight years old and is kind of terrible at the job. They either switch our train to a different track whenever it should be continuing forward (problems with motivation when there's not enough stimulus or reward), OR the switchman isn't even manning their post during those times when we desperately need to be veering off because another train is approaching from the opposite direction. That's the perseveration part. We get fixated and frozen on a path despite warning bells and consequences looming ahead. We vaguely get that we're not on the right course, but what we can see coming is not nearly as in focus or accurate as what we are currently doing or what we imagine might happen.

Interestingly, people on the autism spectrum also have a major tendency towards perseveration. In fact, ADHD and autism spectrum disorder (ASD) have a high rate of comorbidity (occur simultaneously in many people). It's still unclear, though, if the same brain mechanics are involved in the difficulties experienced in ADHD and ASD with inhibiting certain kinds of behaviors.[27]

What is clear is that there is a lot of overlap with the two developmental disorders, including being compelled to repeat mistakes or thought processes and behavior despite changing conditions or evidence of low functionality. These behaviors represent the inability to undertake set shifting (changing of goals, tasks, or activities) as required. Often, we can't seem to make another choice when our first choice proves to be unworkable. We may be particularly obsessed with one line of thinking, even if it's not serving us well. We just

---

[27]Albajara Sáenz, A., Septier, M., Van Schuerbeek, P. *et al.* ADHD and ASD: distinct brain patterns of inhibition-related activation?. *Transl Psychiatry* **10**, 24 (2020). https://doi.org/10.1038/s41398-020-0707-z

keep doing what we're doing, and then we seem surprised when things inevitably turn out the way they do.

How do we get this stuck? Well, we start out with atypicality in our neural circuitry that predisposes us to impaired executive functioning. Then, we top it off with a stress trigger. Studies have shown that everyone's little, almond-shaped amygdala (the emotional center of our brains) is extremely sensitive to stress. Under conditions of stress, the amygdala activates stress signaling pathways to other areas of the brain such as the hypothalamus. As a result, high levels of noradrenaline (NA) and dopamine (DA) get released. This impairs the functioning of the prefrontal cortex, so all the executive functions suffer. These stress hormones also serve to strengthen the amygdala and generate even greater feelings of fear and anxiety. The less control we feel we have over a situation, the more impaired our prefrontal cortex regions become.[28]

No wonder, then, that our tendency towards perseveration and rigidity worsens when we ADHD and ASD-ers have our anxiety triggered. The more out of control we feel, the less cognitively complex tasks we can manage. The prefrontal cortex executive functions become so impaired by the release of stress hormones that the brain switches to more primitive brain circuits to take over the controls of behavior and emotion. We get stuck in simplistic, rigid, one-way thinking and can't shift our focus, consider other viewpoints, or adapt

---

[28] Arnsten AF. Stress "Signaling Pathways That Impair Prefrontal Cortex Structure and Function". Nat Rev Neurosci. 2009 Jun;10(6):410-22. doi: 10.1038/nrn2648. PMID: 19455173; PMCID: PMC2907136.

as situations change. Sadly, without the benefit of complex thinking, we may well be missing an entirely different and much more pressing consequence by focusing on the thing that causes immediate anxiety rather than on more long-term causes and effects. (C'mon, Grandma Toby, my sister and I were playing with actual lethal weapons and you were worried about the dolls losing their clothes!)

The idea that there could be more than one way of doing something successfully, or that another person's command of the situation or viewpoint could make sense and be a valid approach goes right over our heads when we are dysregulated by anxiety. The only solution we can see is the one where others do what we want. Because when we are inflexible and get our way, that feeling of control helps to keep our anxiety in check and gives us more of a shot at emotional regulation.[29] In fact, changing our perception of the situation from one in which we feel out of control to one in which we feel in control is perhaps the only thing that can get us out of a rigid, perseverative state. Having someone tell us to calm down or stop feeling anxious certainly isn't going to do it!

A serious example of my rigidity stemming from deep anxiety happened when my son was an infant. I was bound and determined to breastfeed him because I was well aware of the health benefits of doing so. The problem was that he didn't seem to be getting enough milk from me. I rented a hospital-grade pump to get my milk flowing better, fed him for hours at a time during the day, and got up four times a night to feed

---

[29] Pera, Gina. Is it You, Me, or Adult ADD?. pg. 55

him. Yet still he wouldn't sleep and he had a yellow tinge to his skin. Finally, our nurse practitioner advised us to feed him formula. I was devastated. I had read that once babies began bottle-feeding, they often rejected the breast altogether. I worried excessively about how formula would affect his future. I couldn't let it go. Instead of changing course, I just tried even harder. I pushed myself to complete exhaustion trying to find a solution that fit my rigid ideals, but to no avail.

In the end, Casey ended up having to make me promise that while he was at work I would give our infant son one bottle of formula during the day. Thankfully, this was all our baby needed to begin to sleep better and to put on weight. But for me, making that shift was like when the tin man in the Wizard of Oz has been rusted into one position for years and years before Dorothy finds him, and even though his oil can is right there, it's impossible for him to reach it without help. I was obsessed with one rigid line of thinking, and I couldn't break out of it to see another way forward. Without help, I might have perseverated to the point of causing both myself and our son harm.

When I used to get swept away by my anxiety, stuck in a place where I couldn't objectively assess the situation and regulate my actions and emotions, Casey employed an interesting strategy to calm me down and snap me out of it. We had a pet rabbit, and we had discovered that whenever we stroked his nose from top to bottom, he quickly became relaxed and tranquil. Whenever I was in the middle of spinning out with anxiety-driven language and behavior, Casey used this same technique with me, slowly and deliberately reaching out to stroke my nose, and it worked well as an external cue to get me to reset. It was an accidental discovery that the motion calmed me down.

I didn't know at the time that this repetitive motion that helped me self-regulate was a form of self-stimulatory behavior ("stimming") widely practiced by both ADHD-ers and ASD-ers. Stimming is the repetitive use of gestures or sounds, and can be anything from hand-flapping, to toe wiggling, to leg-shaking, to humming the same bit of a tune over and over. When we are anxious and feeling unregulated, and our primitive brain circuitry kicks in, these repetitive, habitual behaviors can be soothing. We may also stim to focus our attention or to express intense emotions such as excitement or pain. Stimming may look different (or not) in those of us who are ADHD or on the autism spectrum, but the reasons for it are often similar. Fundamentally, stimming brings us into better balance and is a natural tool to help with self-regulation.

Another thing I learned much later was why, like our little rabbit, I seemed to be wired for fear. It turns out there's a biological reason for that fear wiring. New research has demonstrated a correlation between ADHD and Post Traumatic Stress Disorder. It suggests that people with ADHD are at a significantly elevated risk for PTSD, and vice versa. In fact, the relative risk for PTSD in people with ADHD is four times greater compared to normal controls. Apparently, dysfunctional activation of the brain's fear circuitry is implicated in both disorders. Interestingly, irregularities in the neurotransmission of dopamine occur in both disorders, as do common specific genetic risk factors, including polymorphisms (the simultaneous occurrence of two or more variants of a gene) in the dopamine transporter gene and the cannabinoid receptor gene.[30] Broadly speaking, these genes play an important role in the brain's memory formation and recall as well as in its response to anxiety and fear. Since Rejection Sensitive Dysphoria has to do with both *real* and *perceived* rejection, I wonder if our dysfunctional fear circuitry serves to exaggerate our perception of being under attack. Scientists are learning more about the brain every day, but it may take many more years before we have a full understanding.

Scientists do know that one of the crucial factors necessary for getting past trauma is called fear extinction learning (extinguishing a fear over time and replacing it with new associations and memories) Essentially, the brain has a certain ability to heal itself from a fear response. However, the areas of the brain where this learning takes place show dysfunctional activation in individuals with ADHD as well as in individuals with PTSD. It seems that, lacking the regulatory and calming effect of dopamine on specific receptors, the brain's fear circuitry gets stuck on replay. The nervous system remains on high-arousal, triggered by cues related to the preceding traumatic event and unable to regulate its emotional

[30]Spencer, A. E., Marin, M. F., Milad, M. R., Spencer, T. J., Bogucki, O. E., Pope, A. L., Plasencia, N., Hughes, B., Pace-Schott, E. F., Fitzgerald, M., Uchida, M., & Biederman, J. (2017). Abnormal fear circuitry in Attention Deficit Hyperactivity Disorder: A controlled magnetic resonance imaging study. Psychiatry research. Neuroimaging, 262, 55–62. https://doi.org/10.1016/j.pscychresns.2016.12.015

response of intense distress and physiological reactions even when those cues have nothing to do with the original event.

If the hallmark anxiety and emotional hyper-arousal reported by those of us with ADHD is due in part to this genetically inherited dysfunctional fear circuitry, it makes sense how trauma can be passed through the generations. I imagine that my grandfather, already genetically prone to dysfunctional fear circuitry, ended up with PTSD from his single mother having to take him to an orphanage because she couldn't afford to feed him. He perpetuated that abandonment with his own children by being so distracted, restless and dissatisfied with himself that he couldn't offer them the approval and affirmation they needed. My mother, her fear circuitry triggered by something I'd done that took her back to that childhood disapproval from her father, passed those abandonment issues on to me by withdrawing her love and approval via the silent treatment.

Those of us with ADHD and other disorders affecting the brain's frontal lobes generally don't have much self-insight into our behaviors. We may unintentionally hurt ourselves and the people closest to us as a result. Unconsciously, we self-medicate with whatever stimulates our brains, including anxiety and negativity. Both of my grandparents had a negative view of people – his was distrustful; hers was fearful. In fact, they thrived on negativity. Everything was "terrible," "awful," and "horrible." It was them against the world. Toby armored up inside her girdle inside their dark house; Al believed that everyone was out to rip him off. They tended to communicate by shouting at each other:

"Al-*BEAR*-toe! You've been in that basement for three hours!"

"Aw, Toby, shuddup 'da face!"

I've talked about how people with ADHD often stir up conflict because it's a natural stimulant. According to psychiatrist Daniel Amen, "Being mad, upset, angry, negative, or even oppositional immediately stimulates the brain's frontal lobes." These behaviors increase adrenaline, which ultimately stimulates brain activity.[31] Similarly, habitual patterns of negative thinking (focusing only on the bad, and blaming other people and things for our problems), is another unfortunate way of deriving stimulation. The more sensationally awful something turns out to be, the more it generates a sort of perverse satisfaction. We can easily perseverate in negativity as another coping mechanism for unmanaged ADHD, even though it doesn't serve us well, and, even worse, we can pass these habits to the next generation.

---

[31] Amen, Daniel as cited in Pera, Gina. Is it You, Me, or Adult ADD? pg. 94.

8

Time Stops When You're Having Fun

Another way to describe perseveration is called "hyperfocus." Both terms mean having a kind of tunnel vision and dogged focus on one thing to the exclusion of all else. Hyperfocus is a kind of perseveration because we get sucked in and can't manage to switch tasks, even if we know we should. The terms are not entirely synonymous with each other, though. With both perseveration and hyperfocus, we can't inhibit our behavior to stop doing a thing. However, with hyperfocus the reason is because it's so engaging or so high stakes. With hyperfocus, chances are it's leading somewhere and we're doing something efficiently, even if it's not the thing we're supposed to be doing. Perseveration, on the other hand, generally leads to a dead end where our behavior is no longer functional. Yet we are so swept away by the stimulus that we can't adequately problem-solve a better solution.

In the right circumstances, hyperfocus can be more of a superpower than a hindrance. With hyperfocus, we persevere to the extreme because whatever we're doing is particularly captivating for us. It commands all of our attention either because it's so interesting, because it has an immediate deadline linked to dire consequences, or because it's high-stakes (such as working in an emergency room or playing a fast-paced, competitive game). In hyperfocus mode, we are efficient and concentrated. We know exactly what to do next and we are getting it done. Our ADHD symptoms seem to melt away as we get sucked into a place of high interest and our minds feel stimulated with a beautiful intensity. In hyperfocus mode, our dopamine levels rise and we experience the feedback of the brain's reward system.

When we hyperfocus, it doesn't matter where we are. We could be on a plane, in the rain, or, say, on a train. We don't notice anything around us. Our sense of the external world vanishes. What we are doing is of such high interest or high stakes that we don't have the slightest chance of inhibiting our behavior. We have become stimulation swept-away, powerless to resist our response to it. If all our unregulated impulses are a train, we've just entered a time-machine tunnel. In that tunnel that goes on and on, there is no day or night, no hunger or thirst, no physical discomfort or competing demands. The only time is right now, and the only experience is this fascinating thing that soaks up every last particle of our attention. We could be in that tunnel for hours, days, or years.

When we finally emerge into the light of day, we may find that everybody we know has aged considerably while we haven't aged a day, and "Netflix" is no longer a thing. If you've ever looked up to find it's gotten dark outside when you could have sworn it was only 11am, and the first thing you said was "Wait, what time is it?" you know what I'm talking about. Some people refer to the condition of hyperfocus as being "in the zone." It's great when the zone coordinates with a task we're supposed to be doing, or if we are merrily focusing on an interest in our free time. The problem is that we don't control when it happens, and once we're in there, it's practically impossible to get out. Further, sometimes the time-machine tunnel isn't the one we should be entering at all. In fact, sometimes other demands necessitate bypassing the time-machine tunnel altogether, but, I mean, who can resist a time-machine tunnel, right? And so we enter in our unregulated impulse trains and find that there's no way out but forward.

During the Covid-19 pandemic, when schools were about to be shut down, my principal called all the teachers into a meeting and told us that we needed to create ten non-sequential, distance learning lesson plans of review material for each class we taught. I taught four different courses, so that meant I had to create 40 lesson plans, and I was supposed to do it in one day! At 9am, after our faculty meeting, I went into my classroom to work, settling down with my laptop in my chair by the window. I stared out the window at the parking lot for a long time as my thoughts swirled and I tried to figure out where to begin. Typical of my ADHD brain, I began working in all directions at once, trying to utilize too many resources at the same time. I looked back over last year's lesson plans for one class, searched Pinterest for ideas for another class, read snippets of books on various teaching subjects, read plans my colleagues had created, and scribbled down a bunch of random ideas for all classes, in no particular order.

Hours went by, and I still hadn't created any lesson plans. Then, at some point, I got sucked into a hyperfocus tunnel of thinking up creative writing prompts for my 6th graders and analyzing the state Standards of Learning for their grade in order to generate review assignments that met each objective. The Standards of Learning involve about a hundred different things teachers are supposed to accomplish with a course in a year. They are multi-faceted and very detailed. I didn't need to correlate every review assignment to a standard. I just needed to get a bunch of assignments written for my students to do on their own at home.

Another trait of the ADHD brain is that we also tend to underestimate a project's complexity and how long it will take. By going all the way back to the origins of the universe, (aka, the individual Standards of Learning for each grade level), I thought I could lay out a linear path for myself to follow. I was stimulated because it felt really productive and thorough, like I was doing it the "right" way. But this was a far more complex and unsustainable way of putting together my 40 plans, all of which were simply supposed to be a review of material, and it certainly wasn't possible to do in one day.

Nonetheless, it's the path I followed. It was the only way forward I could imagine.

As I worked, I was dimly aware of my classroom phone ringing on my desk across the room a couple of times. I was also dimly aware that I was getting hungrier and hungrier, but these were the only vague indicators that time was passing. I was "in the zone," and my creativity was flowing into my lesson plans. Hours went by. A text from my supervisor finally snapped me out of it. "Where are you? I need to head home and I haven't seen your plans yet." I looked out the window and saw that there were only two cars left in the parking lot. "Wait, what time is it?" I wondered. It was 5pm, and I'd written ten lessons. When my desk phone had rung across the room earlier, that must have been my supervisor calling me. Whoops. When we're in "the zone," we don't see the consequences of our actions looming on the horizon. I knew I shouldn't be approaching the task the way I was, but my issues were multi-faceted:

- Due to deficits with executive functions, I couldn't get a clear sense of a path to take and of which steps to prioritize and which to put off. I just dove in and tried to work in all directions at once.
- Once I was finally able to hone in on something and direct my attention there, I couldn't task switch. I perseverated even though I knew in the back of my mind that it was taking too much time.
- Because the ADHD nervous system is interest-based rather than importance-based, I became engaged with

the stimulus of high-interest material (creative writing prompts) which conversely further diminished my ability to analyze and solve problems such as coming up with an easier solution for getting the work accomplished.

- I couldn't really "feel" the effects of my actions until it was too late because I was swept away in the moment, a classic example of "How'd that happen?"

Because those of us with ADHD take in stimuli through all of our senses more fully and more rapidly than do our neurotypical peers, it's kind of like we are at the whim of our own unregulated impulse trains made up of freight cars with doors stuck wide open. All sorts of soot and sounds are blowing in at high speeds with nothing to help filter them out. Our heads are full of constant chatter, ideas, impulses, emotions, and reactions to what our senses take in. These things are all swirling around mingling with a nagging restlessness, unease, or vague looming sense of doom. Doctor Edward (Ned) Hallowell, a psychiatrist and founder of the Hollowell ADHD Centers for Cognitive and Emotional Health, writes in his famous book *Driven to Distraction*: "People with ADD are always reacting. Even when they look calm and sedate, they are usually churning inside, taking this piece of data and moving it there, pushing this thought through their emotional network, putting that idea on the fire to burn, exploding or subsiding, but always in motion."[32] It doesn't help that our freight cars also have no filing systems. They're just big heavy rectangles with stuff flying in and out of them all day. So, what we take in doesn't get categorized and filed for easy retrieval later. It's all just jumbled in there in messy piles that may or may not blow away. Remind you of your office? Your desk? Your kitchen counter? The side of your bed? Your dining room table?

I have a train problem for you to solve:

At 10:00 AM train A left the station with its doors open, faulty brakes, and black smoke belching from its smokestack. An hour later train B left the same station on a parallel track with its freight cars tightly shut, puffs of white smoke drifting into the air at regular intervals, and a switchman at the ready in the control station. If train A traveled between 120 miles per hour and 5 miles per hour, disappeared into tunnels for between one hour to two days, and retraced its route three times, and train B traveled at a constant speed of 60 miles per hour in a straight line, then how long would it take for train B to pass train A?

In a world where linear thinking is prized, as is concrete, quantifiable output, our neurotypical peers will always pass us. It's really only a question of by how much. It's not all doom

---

[32] Hallowell, Edward M., and John J. Ratey. *Driven to Distraction: Recognizing and Coping with Attention Deficit Disorder from Childhood through Adulthood.* Simon & Schuster, 2011. Pg. 220

and gloom, though. For while train A may not win the race (or even come back at all), what it discovers out there will be like nothing train B, in all its forward moving efficiency, could ever access. Out of randomness, chaos, inefficiency, and stimuli colliding that don't go together blooms creativity. Creativity comes out of nowhere. It's impulsive and doesn't fit in a "proper" place. As Dr. Hallowell points out, "Nowhere is where many ADD people live all the time. Neither here nor there nor anywhere in particular, but rather here and there, not in any one place, but all over the place, nowhere precisely. And it is out of nowhere, on the wings of impulse, that creativity flies in."[33] With us, you never really know what innovative ideas we'll come up with. When I finally did complete my 40 lesson plans (which took two full days, and a great deal of teeth-clenching agony), some of them were remarkably creative. It took me a long time, but I was able to make the teaching relevant to my students' real lives in fresh ways and hit almost all of the Standards of Learning in the process.

---

[33] Hallowell, Edward M., and John J. Ratey. *Driven to Distraction. 220.*

9

Hyperarousal and Impulsivity

ADHD is a neurological disorder. Without intervention, it can lead to some pretty serious consequences: dangerous thrill-seeking, substance abuse, financial ruin, divorce, job loss, low self esteem, anxiety, depression. Part of the problem is that it's such a misnomer that many of us who are struggling in life don't realize it relates to us. For some of us, hyperfocus is our main problem. "Attention Deficit?" Don't be silly. Maybe we are the workaholics who seek and find stimulation in stressful jobs that help to keep the brain aroused and focused (while our families get ignored and feel unloved and unnoticed). Maybe we do parts of our jobs really well because those parts are always changing, challenging and keeping us on our toes, providing us with novelty, but we have problems buckling down and turning in our paperwork. Maybe we are creative and attentive parents, but our spouses or partners feel like we don't hold up our end of the household chores or recognize when things need to get done. We don't have a deficit of attention. We just constantly place it in unusual ways.

All of us with ADHD have difficulties regulating our behavior on a daily basis. We have an interest-based nervous system and low dopamine levels, and that means we aren't motivated by the same things that motivate neurotypical people – namely delayed rewards, importance, or consequences. We often can't get ourselves to do what needs to be done, or in contrast we can't stop doing what we're fully engaged in. We have a hard time controlling our impulses for gratification. Because key components of our brain's reward system are underdeveloped, we choose the lesser, short term rewards that provide us with a quick dose of gratification over the more substantial, longer-term rewards that don't provide enough gratifying feedback to sustain our attention. This poor behavioral inhibition may include problems regulating emotional responses as well, especially as they relate to what is considered socially appropriate behavior.

This is where the subtypes start to come into play. (Though this particular subtyping in diagnosis may be on its way out). Those with the Primarily Inattentive subtype appear to be more absorbed in daydreams and experience mental fogginess and forgetfulness. Most of our difficulties involve selecting what to pay attention to and then sustaining that attention. We may seem passive or sluggish and process information more slowly.

Those of us with the primarily Hyperactive/Impulsive subtype experience difficulties with motivation and regulating our attention as well, but these are compounded by difficulties internalizing our emotions, moderating them so that we don't come off as hot-headed or emotionally immature.[34] We experience a marked degree of hyperarousal, or a sense of internal restlessness. We might also externalize that restlessness and appear fidgety. We feel that we always need to be "doing something," yet when we attempt to accomplish tasks we are a whirlwind that moves from thing to thing, constantly beginning new tasks without completing the earlier ones we started. We have more problems related to impulsivity in social settings. Hence, we make a lot of social gaffes because we don't easily hide what we feel and we have knee-jerk reactions before we are able to stop and think.

According to Dr. Barkley, Savior of the Scattered, the majority of people with ADHD move between subtypes depending upon situation and life experiences at any particular point in time, causing us to be diagnosed with the Combined Type. In fact, he suggests that more research on the Primarily Inattentive subtype might one day position it as an altogether separate disorder from that of ADHD, because almost all of us who have ADHD experience some form of hyperactivity – whether it's externalized or internalized, rather than true sluggishness.

Maybe you're saying to yourself, "Yeah, I was totally that hyperactive kid who couldn't sit still and was touching

---

[34] Barkley, Russell. Fact Sheet: Attention Deficit Hyperactivity Disorder (ADHD) Topics. Russellbarkley.org

everything and bouncing off walls." Or maybe you're saying "I was never like that. I could always sit still for hours." Some of us might even get a little bit indignant that the official acronym is "ADHD" and not just "ADD." Heck, my new keyboard won't even type an "H" half the time. Regardless, if you have ADHD, chances are that "H" almost certainly applies to you in some fashion or another. I always thought I was good at sitting still, but my toes give me away. They insist on wiggling and stretching, quite of their own accord. And they don't like to be stuck in shoes. If I'm going to be sitting for a long period of time, I have to take my shoes off and tuck my legs up under me on the chair. This is another example of the self-stimulatory behavior I talked about earlier. I've noticed that my toes tend to get wigglier when I'm intensely involved in a conversation. I think my toe wiggling expresses my excitement or my emotional engagement. It's also a way for me to discharge the extra energy that builds up when I'm emotionally hyper-aroused.

Your "hyperactivity" might manifest as constant, low-level fidgeting and movement, excessive talking, blurting out, or busy-bodying around the house. It might manifest as well as "hyper-reactivity," meaning excessive emotional responses in your interactions with others. You may have a difficult time regulating your excessive impatience, or your feelings of rejection, or your anger.

As I previously mentioned, hyperactivity in girls often presents in an overly talkative and emotionally reactive way. It's an internal or external restlessness that is so strong, it overpowers our ability to blend in with others in a socially appropriate manner. This restlessness leads some of us to more high-stimulation seeking behavior than others, but the majority of people with ADHD need a certain amount of novelty, several irons in the fire at once, and a fast pace in order to get our neurons firing. Therefore, we tend to get impatient in situations where we have to wait in line for long periods, or sit in a business meeting, or do anything dictated by other people that we don't feel like doing. Almost inevitably, that impatience or restlessness shows up at some point as an impulsive reaction to a stimulus that makes us look a little odd.

One day, many years ago, I had a teaching job at an independent school just a couple of blocks from my house. I was walking to work that morning, and a flash of movement in a tree caught my attention. I looked up and saw a bird hanging upside-down with its feet tangled in some sort of string. It was flapping its wings helplessly as it swung back and forth underneath the branch. Immediately, I went into full-on stimulation swept-away mode.

There was no time to lose. The bird was in crisis. Something had to be done. Any thoughts of my students waiting for me in the classroom 20 minutes from now, or what my department chair would think if I didn't show up for work, weren't even on my radar.

The big oak tree with the desperate bird was in the front yard of an old Victorian that was being used as a fraternity house. I went straight up to the front door and began frantically banging on it. What was my plan, exactly? I didn't have one, of course, but I knew I needed help to save the bird.

It was 7:30 AM and I was banging on the door of a strange fraternity house instead of going to work to teach my students. That's impulsivity for you. This was before the era of cell phones, so I couldn't call my department chair to let her know I'd probably be late. I'm pretty sure I wouldn't have called her even if I *had* had a cell phone, though, because all I could think about in that moment was that bird's suffering. Nothing else in my regular world existed.

After I'd been knocking for several minutes, the large, wooden door finally opened and a weary-looking young man with disheveled hair peered at me out of the gloom of his foyer. I can imagine his confusion at being awakened by insistent knocking and then opening the door to find a young woman in her 20's carrying a briefcase and yelling at him about some bird. My hyperreactive intensity hit him full force: "YOU HAVE TO DO SOMETHING THERE'S A BIRD AND IT'S CAUGHT IN THE STRING YOU HAVE TO SAVE IT RIGHT NOW!" I blurted. I had to say this several times, but finally he looked where I was pointing and sized up the situation. "Let me go get a ladder," he said, and he disappeared.

I will always be grateful to that boy for getting out of bed to answer the door and then for not shutting the door in my face. Of course it didn't occur to me then that he might take any other course of action but to help. I was so caught up in my concern for the bird that naturally I expected everyone else would drop everything to join me.

The young man came out from around the side of his house carrying a rickety-looking, old wooden ladder. I followed behind him like a toy poodle yapping at his heels ("What're you gonna do? Hurry, hurry...") as he walked over to the tree and propped the ladder up against it. Without a word, he climbed up the ladder. When he got close enough to the poor, upside-down bird, he pulled a pocketknife from his pocket. With his left hand holding onto the top rung, he reached out with his right hand and began sawing at the clump of swinging string with the knife. It was a precarious situation with that kind fraternity boy balancing himself high up on the shaky ladder. The tangled bird was flapping violently, and to make matters worse its mate began dive-bombing the young man. One of the only things I remember the young man saying was "AAAGH, it's mate's attacking me!"

By some miracle, the fraternity boy was able to cut the bird loose without falling and breaking his own neck. (Why wasn't I the one to climb the ladder and free the bird, you ask? That ladder was scary, and it was high up, and I wasn't wearing the right shoes. I mean, I had some sense of self-control. Besides, I was dimly aware that fraternity boys are supposed to help old women carry their groceries and stuff. Or is that Boy Scouts? But I digress). The bird flew up into the sky, short lengths of string trailing from its feet. Its mate followed. It was free!

And just like that, I came out of my hyperfocused, impulsive trance. "Wait, what time is it? Oh no, I'm late!" I thanked the young man profusely and rushed off down the street to school. My students had been sitting in the classroom wondering where I was. My department chair had been looking all over for me. She could have fired me. But, I mean, I had to save the bird. What choice did I have? Should I not have done that?

I kick myself all the time for the impulses that get me into situations like this. My lack of foresight and impulsivity make me feel sometimes like I'm careening through my life without those essential brakes to stop me. Dr. Barkley, Savior of the Scattered, writes "If you can't stop your own actions, thoughts, and emotions to give time and self-control a chance to get any traction, you won't be guided to decisions that would be better for your long-term welfare."[35]

In what ways does your freight train of uncontrolled impulses barrel down the track, and what carnage is left in its wake? In a meeting, do you blurt out something without thinking? Do you dominate the conversation or get caught up with a great idea that you can't let go? Maybe you get too loud when you're excited about something, or find it hard to stop talking once you get started. Do you get so caught up in a side conversation with a coworker about salsa dancing that you don't realize you're disrupting the rest of the meeting? Are you impatient when someone else is explaining something? Our restlessness and impulsivity make us want to "cut to the chase," skip the boring stuff and get to the interesting bits, try a little of this and a little of that, jump in with both feet when it's something we care about; jump out the window when it's something we don't.

It all comes back to problems with behavioral and emotional inhibition leading to an inability to exert self-control to guide ourselves towards desired outcomes. When we are in the mode of stimulation swept-away, we can be hyperfocused to the exclusion of all else, look up and go "what time is it?" When we are in the mode of stimulation-avoiding, the bombardment of sensory stimulation is "terrible, awful, and horrible," and we need to shut down or escape. When we are in stimulation-seeking mode, we might be the dangerous thrill-

---

[35] Barkley, Russell. Taking Charge of Adult ADHD. Pg. 53

seeker, the road rager, or the one who gets in trouble at work for knee-jerk reactions or for missing social cues. For many of us, stimulation-seeking mode is when we get into the most trouble, as it's when our impulsivity rears its head in pursuit of feel-good rewards. It might lead to constant rifts with family and co-workers (because conflict is stimulating, plus we get emotionally reactive), problems with addiction or the law, car accidents (eight times more common for those of us with ADHD), and consistently poor judgment and risk-taking.

That's why this chapter is titled "Should I Not Have Done That?" That "H" in ADHD is our restlessness and intensity, our emotional reactivity, our impulse freight train barreling down the tracks with no brakes that keeps us from being able to exercise the self-control we know we ought to have. Only in hindsight do we sometimes recognize the unintended effect we've had on others as a result of our impulsive reactions to our environment.

According to the University of California-Berkeley longitudinal study, the amount of impulsivity is a major predictor for outcomes in girls with ADHD. The risk for serious suicide attempts for girls with the combined inattentive/impulsive type of ADHD was nearly 23% by young adulthood, and rates of moderate to severe non-suicidal self-injurious behavior were over 50%.[36] Put another way, there is a very real threat that being a young adult female with untreated ADHD can cost you your life. There is also a very

---

[36] Hinshaw, Stephen. Understanding girls with ADHD (xvii)

real threat that being a young adult male with untreated ADHD can land you in jail. 26.2% of the adult prison population and 30% of the kids in the juvenile justice system have untreated ADHD.[37] There have been countless times when I get to the end of the day and mentally add up all of the things I've managed to do wrong, all of the people I've inadvertently alienated, or the impressions of me I wish people hadn't formed based on my impulsive behavior. It's exhausting and demoralizing and lonely, and it can lead to a feeling of hopelessness because it seems so much beyond our control.

Fred Rogers, on his show Mr. Rogers' Neighborhood, spent a lot of time helping children learn self-control and self-monitoring. His song "What Do You Do?" is all about resisting impulses:

What do you do with the mad that you feel
when you feel so mad you could bite? When the
whole wide world seems oh, so wrong.
And nothing you do seems very right?

[37] Young S, Moss D, Sedgwick O, Fridman M, Hodgkins P. A meta-analysis of the prevalence of attention deficit hyperactivity disorder in incarcerated populations. Psychol Med. 2015 Jan;45(2):247-58. doi: 10.1017/S0033291714000762. Epub 2014 Apr 7. PMID: 25066071; PMCID: PMC4301200.

What do you do? Do you punch a bag?
Do you pound some clay or some dough?
Do you round up friends for a game of tag?
Or see how fast you go?

It's great to be able to stop
when you've planned a thing that's wrong
and be able to do something else instead
And think – this song:

I can stop when I want to,
I can stop when I wish
Can stop, stop, stop anytime.
And what a good feeling to feel like this
And know that the feeling is
really mine.

Know that there's something
deep inside that helps us become what we can.
For a girl can be someday a woman,
And a boy can be someday a man.

Mr. Rogers knew that in early childhood, children were
developing impulse control. When we are very young, we
depend on our parents and other adults to provide the external
structure that helps us to regulate our impulses. Over time, that
self-control becomes more and more internal as we develop
internal resources like self-talk, internal images, and making
connections between cause and effect. Eventually, we develop

the ability to anticipate and plan for the future with goal-directed behavior. The area of the brain where much of this self-regulating behavior takes place is the left and right prefrontal cortex just behind the forehead.

As I explained earlier, Magnetic Resonance Imaging of the brains of children with ADHD indicate that there is less cortical thickness and a reduced volume of grey and white matter in multiple areas of the brain compared to controls:

> *ADHD children whose symptoms persisted into adolescence had thinner medial prefrontal cortex at an average age of 8.7 years compared to both ADHD children whose symptoms remitted and to controls.*[38]

In addition, the areas where inhibitory and working memory processes take place demonstrate reduced activation in people with ADHD compared to controls:

> *Thus, the bulk of the findings, which are from children and adults, indicate that ADHD is associated with reduced activation of frontal cortex and associated striatal and cerebellar structures during tasks drawing upon executive function.*[39]

---

[38] Shaw P, Lurch J, Greenstein D, Sharp W, Clasen L, Evans A, et al. Longitudinal mapping of cortical thickness and clinical outcome in children and adolescents with attention-deficit/hyperactivity disorder. Arch Gen Psychiatry. 2006; 63: 540-549. [PubMed]. As cited in Vaidya, Chandan J. Neurodevelopmental Abnormalities in ADHD. Curr Top Behav Neurosci. https://www.ncbi.nim/nih.gov/pmc/articles/ PMC3329889/. 4.

Since so many of our ADHD symptoms stem from these issues with executive function maturation and activation, we should go into more detail about what they involve. Dr. Barkley, Savior of the Scattered, explains that the executive functions are "The actions directed at ourselves, the mental activities we engage in when we think about our future and what we should be doing to get there and to make it better."[40] They provide the fuel, all the properly maintained and functioning tracks, and the brakes necessary for our freight trains to chug along on a regular and predictable path. In other words, our self-regulating executive functions allow us to control when we get started, where we are headed, and when we stop.

Optimal Executive Functioning allows for these behaviors:
- Organization: the ability to create and maintain systems to keep track of information or materials
- Planning/prioritizing: the ability to create steps to reach a goal and to make decisions about what to focus on
- Set Shifting/flexibility: the ability to change strategies or revise plans when conditions change
- Working memory: the ability to hold information in mind and use it to complete a task
- Impulse control: the ability to stop and think before acting

---

[39] Vaidya, Chandan J. Neurodevelopmental Abnormalities in ADHD. Curr Top Behav Neurosci. https://www.ncbi.nim/nih.gov/pmc/articles/PMC3329889/. 7.
[40] Barkley, Russell. Taking Charge of Adult ADHD. Pg. 68

- Emotional control: the ability to manage feelings by thinking about goals
- Self-monitoring: the ability to monitor and evaluate our own performance
- Task initiation: the ability to recognize when it is time to get started on something and begin without procrastinating[41]

With optimally developed Executive Function capacities, we can manage time because we can recognize how long things will take in its linear flow and plan accordingly. We can put our attention on things, even if they're not interesting, and we can switch focus (tracks) if something else requires our attention or if our current plan of action isn't productive. We can remember details, holding and turning them in our working memory to make use of them. We formulate, plan, and carry out goals from one step to the next instead of working from the middle outwards in all directions. We use hindsight (past experiences) to plan for the future. And we can summon the motivation to successfully accomplish goals in the absence of external direction or structure.

Unfortunately, because ADHD is a developmental disorder, each set of skills that makes up our overall executive functioning is lagging behind our same-age non-ADHD peers, leaving the adult with ADHD often appearing more "childish" and immature than others. We are that little kid in the midst of

[41]National Center for Learning Disabilities | *Executive Function 101* | © 2013 National Center for Learning Disabilities, Inc.

our bigger peers who never seems to hit a growth spurt. Parts
of our brains are smaller and less developed:

> *ADHD children who were not medicated between 12.5
> and 16.4 years showed more rapid cortical thinning. A
> "thinner" cortical mantle relative to control children
> reflects reduced amounts of glial, neuronal, vascular,
> and synaptic processes that comprise the cortex, and is
> interpreted as reflecting less cortical maturation."*[42]

We literally have delayed maturation of areas of our brains that
regulate much of what people think of as "mature" behavior!
We make messes, we have to be reminded what to do, we're
late, we don't accomplish what we should, we're terrible at
cleaning our rooms, we mismanage money, engage in stupid,
risky behavior, or say things we shouldn't. We lose stuff, we
don't listen, we're oblivious, we don't think ahead, we make
others pick up after us, we make impulsive decisions (or can't
make decisions at all).

On the plus side, we can be so FUN! Dr. Hallowell
points out that "We who have ADD often get called out for
being too silly, zany, inappropriate, and over-the-top-to meet
the demands of daily life"[43] Yet, he also praises our originality
and creativity: "I praise silly, irrelevant, tangential, foolish,

---

[42] Vaidya, Chandan J. Neurodevelopmental Abnormalities in ADHD. Curr Top
Behav Neurosci. https://www.ncbi.nim/nih.gov/pmc/articles/PMC3329889/. 4.
[43] Hallowell, E. (2022, April 11). Copyright © 1998 - 2023 WebMD LLC. All
rights reserved. In Praise of the ADHD Funny Bone. ADDitudemag.com.
https://www.additudemag.com/how-to-be-funny-adult-adhd

slapdash, and spur-of-the-moment. I praise the ADHD funny bone. Why? Creativity begins in a mess."

After all, how many other middle-aged people do you know who impulsively ride their carts through Costco or climb a tree to show their child how easy it is (and then can't get down), or drop everything in order to go to New York City on a whim just to do a scavenger hunt (more on this later). Romantic comedies are full of people like us, sprinkling playfulness and joie de vivre into the lives of the focused and efficient. Sure, our eccentric ways and not entirely socially acceptable comments might make us lose our jobs or relationships, but if we could harness the power of the "H," using it prudently, can you just imagine how the world would fall in love with us? Our original ways of seeing and interacting with the world are refreshing to our neurotypical peers (that is, until they're irritating).

With delayed maturation in the area of self-regulation, we ADHD adults may have to write our own song about how difficult it is to STOP, to resist an impulse, and to choose a different course of action. Here is my song for the ADHD-ers:

Why is it True?

Why is it true that when I'm having fun
and the whole wide world is my friend
When I'm happy and free and feeling good about me,
there's something else that MUST get done?

I can't stop when I want to
I can't stop when I wish
Can't stop stop stop though I try
I say the wrong thing and feel really bad
and sometimes I even start to cry.

Know that there's something deep in my brain
That makes me follow white rabbits
It's one thing to know what I should do
but quite another to break these habits.

I can't stop when I want to
but I'll do what I can
I'll cover my mouth if I must.
Or imagine a key turning off the TV –
the one in my head that comes between us.

For my task is to find the help that I need
and yours is to be-lieve -in me.

I wish I could sing this song every time my impulses
hijack me and take me down a set of tracks into a place I didn't
mean to go (only, of course, when it turns out badly. Like
when I crash the Costco cart into the bulk peaches). Often,
our impulses stem from the attempt of our brains to calm our
inner restlessness. In bouncing from task to task, topic to
topic, wall to wall, concentration to impatience, stimulation to
stimulation, we are searching for peace. Wouldn't it be nice to

have a sense of feeling right and calm inside? Instead, we spend a lot of time looking behind us and picking up pieces, sweeping up broken glass, and apologizing. In fact, apology is a great art for us to master. We may find ourselves repeating this phrase to our graves: "I'm sorry, should I not have done that?"

10

Problems with Motivation
and Multiple Steps

Not only is there all the stuff we *shouldn't* do and *shouldn't* say that we're constantly having to navigate and apologize for. But there's also all the stuff we *should* do, yet can't seem to make ourselves do, that weighs upon us on a daily basis. If I have three free hours and there's one thing I absolutely have to do – pay a bill, return a library book, make dinner, empty the dishwasher, water the plant that looks like it's on death's door – I will not only NOT get that one thing accomplished, but I will instead embark with great commitment on a project that takes far more than three hours, and then abandon it six hours in when I realize that I haven't eaten all day and I'm dreadfully late picking up my child from school/camp/tae kwon do. Even when I'm dead and buried

I'll probably still be deluding myself that any day now I'll get around to things I've left unfinished/untouched/untapped/unearthed. Let's look at some examples:

1. An entire corner of my bedroom is given over to summer clothes cascading out of their storage bin in a messy heap because it's August and I've been living out of the bin all summer instead of putting the clothes in the dresser. I was gonna do that.

2. There is only one space at the dining room table for anyone to eat because the rest of the table has been covered for weeks with binders of materials and research books about teaching writing that I need to read. I was gonna do that.

3. There's been no toilet paper in the house for three days and I've been wiping with paper napkins. I really need to get some, like, three days ago. I was gonna do that.

4. I have a bill I need to put into the mail, and it's my second notice with the big red lettering at the top. I was gonna do that.

5. The carpet in my office is covered in cat urine from my dead cat. (She wasn't dead at the time). There's a warranty on it (it's fairly new), but first it needs to be professionally cleaned, or possibly burned. Every time I

work in my office it's like working in a latrine. I was gonna do that.

Why can't I put my mind to it, make the time, take the effort to do fairly simple tasks that would make me feel so much better if they were accomplished? Why do I go to elaborate measures, adding double or even triple to my workload, exhausting myself in the process, just to keep from doing what I have to do?

One major reason is that people with ADHD have problems with poor self-motivation, or task initiation. This is the flipside of our inner restlessness and out of control full-speed-ahead impulses. The fact is, that many times our uninhibited automatic impulse freight trains simply won't budge at all. Or, they'll budge, but only by veering off on a track other than the one they are supposed to be on, and then they pick up speed. Self-motivation is the "Ability to do what needs to be done, without influence from other people or situations. People with self-motivation can find a reason and strength to complete a task, even when challenging, without giving up or needing another to encourage them."[44] Sounds simple, right?

People with ADHD, however, often feel like what *needs* to get done (but is boring or overwhelming) is at the top of a giant hill, and somehow we are supposed to get to the top of it with our impossibly heavy impulse freight trains that have

---

[44] businessdictionary.com

exactly the *wrong* kind of fuel for the journey. Plus, did I mention that the whole track is covered in a thick layer of mud? Our difficulties with task initiation are due to several factors:

1. Lack of interest
2. Inability to see clearly the individual parts of the task and to determine a sequence for them
3. Inability to picture in our "mind's eye" what the task should look like once it's completed, and hence inability to derive any reward from picturing the end result.
4. An inner restlessness that wants to get going on something it can do easily, NOW. (Even if that's just cleaning the toilet, or making a recipe, or washing the dog).

We are fueled by an interest-based nervous system that craves engagement, clarity, and immediate rewards. How are we supposed to start something we aren't excited about? When we aren't interested in something, we literally can't even figure out how to begin. And even if we do "the thing," what are we going to get out of it in return? Certainly no gratification we can imagine right now. Explains Durall, "If a task [such as paying bills] lacks immediate, external incentives, then there will be a resultant lack of arousal, motivation, and persistence. If a task is deemed of little importance or is too distant into the future, then the performance of the ADHD person drops dramatically." [45] If we want to accomplish low-interest tasks, therefore, we need lots of external guidelines, structures, and incentives to get us moving and keep us on track.

This may mean getting help to break down the task into smaller pieces so we can better see where to start. It might mean setting up deadlines and accountability for different stages of the task. We may need to "body double" with other individuals who are also working on their own necessary tasks at the same time (i.e. an adult "study hall"). And we're definitely going to need immediate, tangible rewards all along the way. We could reward ourselves with a quick walk outside once we gather all the materials we need to start the task. Then reward ourselves again once we've worked on it for 15 minutes. And so on. Eventually, we'll find that we've gotten into a groove and can sustain our attention on the task for a longer period.

Sometimes, all that revving of our engine without the proper fuel to get moving sends us spinning off in an entirely different direction. We can manage to summon energy (because we are internally restless and always looking for places to put that restlessness), but we still can't manage to place it on the thing at hand. We cast about like a trapped animal looking for an escape, and we find we suddenly know exactly how to get started with a different project we'd been meaning to do. We throw ourselves into this alternative task wholeheartedly, desperate for those feel-good chemicals in our brains to kick in as we work hard on this noble pursuit. The immediate

---

[45] Durall. Towards an Understanding of ADHD.

gratification of finally getting the dog washed or the dryer vent cleaned out completely erases the looming consequences of not doing the more important task.

Going back to the train analogy, it might look something like this: Just as we're desperately sinking in the mud unable to find a solution for how to get our trains running up that steep hill, a mirage appears. Look, over there, it's a downhill track! And on that track are other things we've been meaning to get done but somehow couldn't do before. Suddenly they don't look so impossible. I mean, at least we'd be getting SOMETHING useful done, right? And then we'd feel so accomplished. OR maybe that downhill track is slickly laid with some wonderful thing that attracts our interest. We'll just mosey on over to the downhill track and peer down there. Suddenly we have motivation, and whoops, our impulse trains are off and running and there's NO turning back. "Wrong way!" we scream to ourselves. But hey, at least we found some momentum (a balm for our inner restlessness). Our trains, fueled either by unregulated internal impulses for pleasurable and interesting stimuli or immediate (and generally dire) external consequences, refuse to start up just because we tell them to, but boy do they like taking us (and often the people closest to us) for a ride!

Another reason our performance may drop dramatically is if a task requires numerous steps in order to complete. Our ADHD brains have a leak in them when it comes to another one of the executive functions, our working memory. Because you may have forgotten what that is by now here is a definition: "Working memory is the ability to have data available in one's mind, and to be able to manipulate that data to come up with an answer or a plan of action."[46] In our case, when we attempt to hold multiple pieces of information or tasks in our mind's eye, they tend to get lost in a black hole. We can't seem to sustain a strong mental image of information and use it to guide our actions. The ADHD brain has a hard time re-seeing and re-hearing information and experiences. Essentially, "information and memories that are out of sight are out of mind." It was those childhood trivia games that taught me I had a problem in this area.

When I try to hold several steps in my mind at once, they shift and disappear. It's like trying to work with smoke rings. This is why long, complicated tasks, math word problems, and shopping lists are so impossible to remember and complete. A task that needs to be broken down into a number of steps is like playing Candyland. I can't stay on a linear progression. I'm going along from colored square to colored square when I get distracted by "chocolate mountain" and forget where I am on the path; or I get mired in "licorice lagoon" and lose a turn; or I get almost to the end when all of a sudden I draw the cupcake card and have to go back to the beginning. The sequence of cards is random, and where I am at any particular point in the process keeps shifting.

---

[46] Dodson, William. (2023, Oct. 23). © 1998 – 2023 WebMD LLC. All rights reserved. Secrets of the ADHD Brain: Why we think, act, and feel the way we do. Additude Magazine. New Hope Media, New York, NY. 2016. Pg. 11

Story #5 from the beginning of this chapter is a perfect example of how a multi-step task doesn't get accomplished. My office carpet is covered in cat pee. The rug stinks. There are many steps involved to make it stop stinking. I can think through and hold in mind the first few of them:

1. Clean it myself (didn't work)

2. Find the warranty in my piles of papers to see if it covers pet stains (it does)

3. Call the people who installed the carpet and ask how to get it replaced under warranty (I did).

It was after I talked to the carpet company that things started to get fuzzy. They listed more steps I needed to go through. I had to take pictures and email them; I needed to clean the carpet with vinegar and water extraction; if that didn't work I needed to have it professionally cleaned, get a receipt, and then call them back; If the stains still didn't come out, they would schedule a time for someone to come and assess the damage in person. Then there would be more steps after that.

After I hung up, I called around for estimates from carpet companies, I checked Groupon ads, and I narrowed down my list of who to call for a cleaning. But each step required decision-making and I started to derail as other possible steps presented themselves. Do I go with the "green," more expensive carpet cleaner, or the cheaper people who use chemicals? Do I buy a $69 Groupon for a company that may or not be reputable, or do I pay $200 for a company that comes with good recommendations? How will I get my furniture moved out of the room? Will I have to pay someone to do that? Who will I pay? Where will the money come from? (I'm a teacher, for God's sake). My ability to hold in mind and follow through on the steps fizzled out. I lost track of what direction to move in. Everything just sort of collapsed in on itself. I never got around to doing the vinegar. I never hired anyone. I really *was* gonna do that. But here I sit, typing away in a room that almost a year later still smells like my dead cat (rest her soul).

I challenge you to make a list right now of five things you were "gonna" do. Can you note next to each one what has kept you from accomplishing the task? Did you do something different instead? Which one have you been meaning to do for the longest time? What do you imagine it would take to get you to do it? Our "I was gonna's" pile up over a lifetime, and the spark of motivation to get them done regularly eludes us.

11

Problems with Mental Images and Working Memory

Our leaky working memory creates problems with ordering and sequence. The ability to move smoothly from one thing to the next in linear sequence is like having a railroad bridge connecting each gap between steps in the task. Those bridges should allow our freight trains to chug safely across each chasm. Our ADHD brain trains, unfortunately, have missing and broken railroad bridges. We are not linear thinkers who see tasks in terms of a beginning, middle, and end. Our world is curvilinear where past, present, and future all combine into right now. "People with ADHD live in a permanent present and have a hard time learning from the past or looking into the future to see the inescapable consequences of their actions."[47] These are the far-reaching impacts of not being able to visualize and manipulate mental images for any length of time. It means we struggle to sort out and organize our thinking (what to do first, next, and so on) and we struggle to get a good view of the future. Dr. Barkley, Savior of the Scattered, calls ADHD a kind of "time blindness" because time and linear sequence have so little meaning for us.[48]

If our mental images keep going up in smoke before we have a chance to act with them in mind, we will be hard-pressed to notice that the last railroad bridge we crossed was a little wobbly and to remember to look far enough ahead with our binoculars to inspect the next railroad bridge for rusted-through tracks before we plunge into the valley below. It's another reason we struggle with an understanding of cause and effect. (Like, I won't have any lesson plans done if I use all my free time to write this book in my reeking of cat pee home office, and that will cause the beginning of the school year to be a miserable, stressful experience... is something I'm just not really "feeling" right now. Instead, the high stimulation I'm getting from writing this book, and the rewarding hit of dopamine that goes with it, has me completely at its mercy).

Gina Pera says "Poor working memory disconnects cause from effect, impairing the ability to predict and prepare for outcomes."[49] My past actions just aren't out there on the table and accessible for me to use in future planning. As soon

---

[47] Dodson, William. Secrets of the ADHD Brain: Why we Think, act, and feel the way we do.

[48] Barkley, Russell. Taking Charge of Adult ADHD. Pg. 56

[49] Pera, Gina. Is it You, Me, or Adult A.D.D.? (50)

as things happen, my memory of them gets buried somewhere under a big old pile. Therefore, any linear connection in my mind of my past actions to my future actions is extremely weak.

So, here we are, the unwitting conductors of our own impulse freight trains fueled by high interest/stimulation or immediate and dire consequences. Our working memory goes up in smoke as a byproduct of the inefficient burning process of our woefully inadequate fuel (In reality, a lack of sufficient neurotransmitters and receptors), which means that we can't easily access and examine what we've already done and learned in order to look ahead and predict and plan for outcomes of our choosing. We aren't hurtling down the tracks from past to future in a straight path; rather, the tracks are all twisted up and crossing each other. Sometimes our trains are headed back the way they came, covering the same ground over and over again. Sometimes we come to a missing railroad bridge and plunge off the end of the tracks, only to fall onto a different track twisting steeply down a mountain. Can you visualize that mental image? Hold it in mind as long as you can.

Now, how long can you hold this one in mind?

"At 10:00 AM train A left the station and an hour later train B left the same station on a parallel track. If train A traveled at a constant speed of 60 miles per hour and train B traveled at 80 miles per hour, then at what time did train B pass train A?"

This is an actual former GRE question used by many online learning sites. Apparently it's pretty straightforward to figure out. If you're an ADHD-er with working memory issues, though, even with pencil and paper you may find it quite difficult. How hard is it for you to manipulare the mental image and parse the problem into what it's really asking and the steps required to solve it? If you have ADHD, you might find yourself just gazing at your working memory smoke rings and humming a tune to yourself with no idea how to get started.

In the ADHD world, with leaky working memory, poor motivation for low interest tasks, and a tendency to tackle a problem by jumping in and working in all directions at once, Train A and Train B would have crashed into each other at exactly 2pm.

But back to my cat-pee rug story: as the sequence of steps for replacing the cat pee rug became more and more complicated to visualize and sort through in my mind, I became increasingly restless and frustrated. Even when I wrote down each step I needed to accomplish, my mind couldn't keep them in a distinct, doable progression. Each step became a magnet for other bits of things that clung to it. For example, cleaning the carpet with vinegar meant having to locate the vinegar and having to find a bucket. The vinegar was under the kitchen sink where I was reminded that I should tuck some more steel wool around the pipes to keep out the mice.

Then I remembered the mice had been in the garage where I needed to go for a bucket. I got caught up in the mouse memories and the feelings they brought up; I got to the garage and saw a toy that I'd been meaning to donate; I felt guilty that I'd let it sit there taking up room for so long (emotional hyperreactivity); I remembered I needed rice vinegar for a recipe and momentarily considered going to the grocery store. Then, somewhere along the way, in a perfect example of escape behavior (that's the part where we metaphorically jump out the window when overstimulation or understimulation gets too intolerable), I thought "Why not paint the mud room?"

I could justify allowing myself to veer off on this new track because it was one of those projects that I really had been meaning to get to. In truth, what was happening was that I was unable to be productive where I needed to be (because I was getting bored and I couldn't filter out unnecessary sensory input and stick to one step at a time), so I went into stimulation-seeking mode for something to replace that task with in order to achieve a feeling of accomplishment and soothe my restless and frustrated soul. If I painted the mudroom, I would be able to forget all about the original task as my hard work was rewarded with the gratification of seeing the fresh paint transform the walls.

I filled up my impulse train with fuel (the motivation of avoidance, plus the restless need to feel productive, plus the stimulation-seeking desire for instant gratification) and began chugging merrily up the hill towards my highest point of interest --getting to see what the walls would look like in a different color. There was no room in my agenda for painting preparation. There were no scheduled train stops at the hardware store for things like choosing a paint color or buying good equipment. I wanted to get to the reward as soon as possible.

I also lacked the working memory to visualize in my mind's eye the full consequences of going to the basement, looking at my stack of half-empty cans of paint, and choosing one I had used in the garage in 2013. In that moment, I was utterly unable to recall and learn from the memory of years before when I had chosen to paint our living room Doritos orange. Instead, I barreled down the track, working myself far harder than necessary painting with old rollers and brushes that weren't up to the task, all because I had too much momentum to stop and do it the right way. I finally ended up with a shiny, freshly painted mudroom in the colors of avocado green and "celery." Then I regretted the avocado color and decided I couldn't stand more than one wall of it. Then I sanded and primed over the very color I had just painted.

In my mudroom example, I expended a ridiculous amount of effort using sub par materials on entirely the wrong project in an impulsive stimulation-seeking move to avoid one boring and longer-term task by being productive in another faster, more immediately gratifying one. I didn't plan ahead or think through my choices using past experience to guide me, and then I was surprised by the resulting disappointment in the colors I used.

It goes back to my song lyrics: "I can't stop when I want to/I can't stop when I wish/can't stop, stop, stop, though I try..." We neither have full control of our braking mechanism nor of the track we are on. Because of our problems with perseveration, many of us can't let go of an idea or topic of conversation even when it is no longer relevant. Or, we make ourselves crazy spinning our brains on a problem without the ability to stop and look at it from a different angle. Or, we paint a wall a color we don't like with old brushes that shed into the paint and STILL we carry on, cause and effect be damned.

12

Out of Sight, Out of Mind

My ex-husband used to get so frustrated when I didn't do the things he wanted me to do. He tried writing deadlines for me on the white board in the hallway. I saw them every day, but deadlines don't work very well for people who don't know the current date, don't have any real sense of how much time has passed, and aren't motivated by external demands. Finally, he resorted to what he referred to as "lighting a fire" under me. He threatened dire consequences generally having to do with abandonment (triggering my Rejection Sensitive Dysphoria). When he put it that way, I was much more likely to hold up my end and "get to it."

According to Dr. Barkley, Savior of the Scattered, "fast-moving events light up the neurotransmitters of the ADHD brain and focus attention."[50] This is why my husband's "fire-lighting" trick worked so well. He instinctively realized that I would, for whatever reason, only perform under stress and high-intensity, so he gave it to me. Says Dr. Barkley, "ADHD leaves you depending on immediate rewards or threats of consequences imposed by others." If those rewards or consequences are too far in the future, though, they are much less effective as motivators. For example, since Casey worked full time and I worked part-time, I knew he expected me to empty the dishwasher before he got home from work. I also knew that he would be angry and take it as a sign that I didn't care about him if I didn't do this job. I wanted to avoid at all costs the terrible feeling of abandonment I'd have if Casey got angry, shut down, and gave me that look where he pressed his lips together into a thin line, triggering me immediately to be transported back to my childhood as I pleaded with my mom to show me her love.

The problem was that I still couldn't seem to empty the dishwasher until the consequences I feared were right in front of me. Throughout the day, I reminded myself that I needed to empty the dishwasher. But my brain always hijacked the situation, choosing a higher stimulation activity with the promise that we still had time and would do the job later, and then forgetting about it altogether. My working memory couldn't keep the task in mind for very long (out of sight, out

---

[50] Barkley, Russell. Taking Charge of Adult ADHD.

of mind), and my stimulation-seeking meant that something more interesting kept derailing my best laid plans.

The time for my husband to arrive home grew ever closer. At 5:00pm, I suddenly remembered, "I need to empty the dishwasher," yet I still couldn't put aside (switch tracks) whatever other task I was engaged in and summon the motivation to take out a dish. Routinely, it wasn't until his car was pulling into the driveway that I suddenly found myself able to fling the china into the cabinets, motivated by intense anxiety. When it was right in front of me how unbearable my husband's rejection would feel, it finally got my neurotransmitters firing. Why couldn't I conjure that image earlier? Why couldn't I see it coming and plan to avoid it completely? I mean, I wasn't exactly caught by surprise. Let's put it all together with everything we've learned so far.

1. My ADHD brain didn't have enough dopamine available to motivate it to do the low-interest task until the stakes were high enough and the consequences immediate.
2. My ADHD brain was receiving pleasurable dopamine from other, more stimulating activities.
3. My leaky working memory couldn't hold the task in mind throughout the day, so I kept forgetting it was even a task to do as other things grabbed my attention. (out of sight, out of mind)
4. My leaky working memory had trouble conjuring up past experiences of what happened when I

didn't empty the dishwasher, and using that feeling to motivate me ahead of time. (i.e. when this happened before, I felt this way, so I should plan not to let that happen again).

5. My ADHD brain had difficulty planning for the task because its organizational system isn't linear. It has trouble doing one thing at a time, prioritizing based on importance, and keeping track of time.

It's overwhelming, paralyzing, and demoralizing to struggle so hard to accomplish simple things that neurotypicals do without a second thought. I wish those things my ex-husband wanted from me hadn't been so crucial to him and his ability to appreciate and respect me. I wish he hadn't taken personally my inability to get things accomplished that he cared about. I wish we had both understood the undertow of ADHD and the ways it was holding me back. Emotional bullying doesn't feel too good even when it's the only apparent option for getting someone to do what you want.

A lighter example of being unable to direct my behavior towards a particular action until the consequences were imminent happened very recently, as I was typing this book. I kept getting a warning on the screen that said "mouse batteries low." Because I was engaged in hyperfocus, happily typing away as ideas flooded my brain, I didn't pause to consider the consequences of my mouse batteries running out. I didn't consider when it might happen or whether I had any new batteries to replace them. I didn't consider the interruption to my work or the fact that I might not have saved recently and wouldn't be able to when the mouse quit. Because the consequences weren't immediate, the impending disruption had little impact on my thought process, other than a vague plan of "I'm gonna do that." So, when the mouse suddenly quit working and I hadn't clicked "Save," and I was midway through typing a thought, and I was caught off-guard, I was irrationally like "How'd that happen?"

I wanted to keep writing, but there were no more AA batteries in the house. I could have made a special trip to the drugstore, but, well, the steps involved in gathering my purse and keys, putting on my shoes, going to the car, and driving somewhere were insurmountable. Instead, I put the batteries in the recharger and waited for hours until they were at full power again. But hey, while I waited at least I emptied the dishwasher.

There are so many other examples of times when I dropped the ball because something was out of sight and I forgot all about it until the consequences were immediate. I'm sure you could make your own list as well. Here are a few more of mine with some blank lines for you to fill in your own:

- Burning something on the stove because I turned it on and then walked away and forgot all about it
- Making my clothes moldy because I put them in the wash and then forgot to take them out
- Turning on the soaker hose in the garden and forgetting it was on until several hours later when water was cascading onto the driveway from the raised beds

- Forgetting to pick up a prescription and then forgetting to take the prescription
- forgetting I have certain online accounts, or forgetting the passwords to online accounts, or forgetting to pay an e-bill because there was no visible record of it
- Going to the Farmer's Market and forgetting the dog was in his crate in the back seat. Running back to the hot car 45 minutes later in an absolute panic when something suddenly triggered my memory that I'd left him there. (Thankfully, he was OK).

Your ball drops:

13

Misremembering and
Revisionist History

I often had trouble in my marriage with remembering details accurately. Casey and I would have a conversation where we agreed to do something or we made some sort of decision, and then I'd forget it. Casey took to writing me follow-up emails after important conversations to help us stay on the same page about our plans. Sometimes he'd remind me of something I could have sworn we'd never talked about, and then he'd show me the email where he'd documented our exchange.

Me: You never told me you were going to a hockey game this weekend.

Casey: Yes, I did. Remember you said you were going to use that time to get work done?

Me: No, you definitely didn't tell me about your plans. (Casey shows me the calendar where he's put the event as well as the email where he forwarded me a copy of his agenda).
Me: Oh.

After a while, the evidence of my forgetfulness was so overwhelming that I stopped trusting in my own experience of events. When I got angry at Casey or felt like he wasn't treating me fairly, it was impossible to stand up for myself because he was the one writing our history. I guess it didn't happen the way I thought it did. He had to be right. After all, look at all the times I misremembered. Not only did I stop trusting my memory of our interactions, but I stopped trusting my feelings, too. If I was upset by something that happened between us and I brought it to Casey's attention, it turned out that it was my behavior that had caused the issue. Somehow these arguments always ended with me apologizing and feeling grateful that Casey was there to set me straight. He was so good, and even-keeled, and objective. It was me and my faulty perspective that was the problem. The history books really are written by the victors, aren't they?

I admit it must be endlessly frustrating for our partners and friends when they are relying on the results of a conversation we've had together and then we either

1. Don't remember the conversation at all
2. Misremember the conversation, or
3. Remember only half the conversation, the part where they are supposed to do something for us.

They think we've come to a clear understanding about something together, only to find the entire foundation of that understanding is built on a sink-hole. They make plans, work towards desired outcomes, and follow their linear life progression thinking we are right behind them and we've got their backs. Whoops. Sorry. This is why I've learned never to make promises or commitments of any kind. Because I know how high the likelihood is that I won't follow through. If I don't immediately add it to my Google calendar with two audible reminders, forget about it.

In the end, it feels like we have no choice about whose perspective to trust. But what if our counterpart is manipulating the facts? What if *they're* not trustworthy, *either,* for different reasons. I think that those of us who struggle a lot with these kinds of working memory problems are more vulnerable to gas-lighting. In this power move, the manipulator makes the other person feel like they're crazy for having their particular point of view. The manipulator's point of view is the only valid one, the only accurate representation of reality. The other person's feelings and concerns are subsumed under this objective truth.

Gas-lighting "...works to distort and erode your sense of reality; it eats away at your ability to trust yourself and inevitably disables you from feeling justified in calling out abuse and mistreatment."[51] Since my ADHD brain really does lead me sometimes into inaccurate perceptions, forgetting what

---

[51] Arabi, Shahida. Power: Surviving and Thriving After Narcissistic Abuse: A Collection of Essays on Malignant Narcissism and Recovery from Emotional Abuse. Thought Catalogue, ed. 2017.

was said, or not hearing everything, I easily become prone to gas-lighting myself and calling into question my own reality. With gas-lighting, "Two conflicting beliefs battle it out; is this person right or can I trust what I experienced? A manipulative person will convince you that the former is an inevitable truth while the latter is a sign of dysfunction on your end."[52]

One instance of Casey completely invalidating my feelings occurred the night before we took our son on vacation to Hawaii. Casey had a work trip right before our vacation, so he left me to pack, set the house in order, and make my way with our son to a hotel in D.C. where we would meet up with him and spend the night before our early morning flight out of Dulles the next day. He instructed me to pack our pop up beach tent into his golf bag, bring the travel car seat in another bag, and pack clothes/toys/beach stuff for me and our son. In addition, of course, there was laundry, dealing with food in the fridge, trash and recycling, dishes, and all the other stuff that goes into leaving a house for an extended period of time.

Of course, due to my (as yet undiagnosed) ADHD, I couldn't really see everything I had to do clearly, and I didn't leave enough time to do it all. I packed, and hauled heavy bags to the car, and cleaned, (and fed and entertained Leo at the same time) until I couldn't see straight. By the time I had driven the three hours to D.C. to meet up with Casey, I was utterly exhausted and furious that Casey had left me to do everything. After we put Leo to bed in the hotel room that night, I remember sitting on the couch in the adjoining room

---

[52]Ibid.

trying to tell Casey how much work I'd done to get ready for our trip and how exhausting it was to do it all on my own.

I guess I was hoping for validation, empathy, maybe even an apology that he'd been away and unable to help. Gratefulness and appreciation would have been nice, too. Instead, he just looked at me coldly. The more emotions I expressed, the less moved he seemed. I remember thinking "Wait, are you angry with me? Do you think I did something wrong? Is it not OK to ask for some understanding and compassion here?" I couldn't figure out why he refused to acknowledge the hard work I'd put in. I wanted to be seen for what I'd done, but he refused to see it. And since he, apparently, wrote our history, it was as if my contributions never happened. To me, getting ready for a big trip all on my own while also taking care of a young child was a big deal. To Casey, I guess it wasn't. Maybe he saw no reason to validate me because in his mind it was all easy.

So much about ADHD causes us to question whether we can really trust our own inner guidance. I realize that I miss things other people see, but I also notice things others don't. It seemed awfully fishy to me that Casey's reality didn't appear to have any empathy in it for how I experienced the situation. His "reality" involved judgment and expectation that I see things his way. Could my experience of how it happened be so "off" that it merited complete dismissal? Was I living in a parallel universe? In his reality, I should be ashamed of myself because my anger/ tears/ feelings caused his unhappiness. In my reality, he abandoned me every time I reached out for some kind of acknowledgment that the way I saw it mattered.

Here's the thing: we do matter. The way we see the world isn't "wrong." Our feelings are still real and justifiable even if our perceptions aren't always spot-on. Because our memories are tied to our emotions, maybe they get even closer to the truth. Who knows?

I'm not gonna lie, divorcing your hard drive leaves quite a gap in your memories of the past. But it's also freeing to realize that history isn't set in stone. It's fluid depending on what you choose to focus on. And there's no such thing as one objective truth.

14

Transforming Our Dissatisfaction with Ourselves

Some ADHD experts say it's important not to think of our ADHD as a neurological disorder or as a disability. It's not an excuse for bad behavior, and we aren't disabled, they say. We are just "neurodiverse" and we should look at all the positive gifts we bring to the world. Yes, exactly, we totally should be proud of our gifts. It's not fair that we have to keep coming up against societal values for work and family life that prize the very things we struggle with the most (executive functions) and disregard and denigrate the things we're best at (nonlinear thinking, empathy and compassion, spontaneity, surprising connections). However, the reality is that we have to function in this world, and therefore in this world ADHD is very much a disorder, a disability, and often a liability.

My partner, Ben, has some hearing loss. It's a daily occurrence for people to be frustrated with him because he can't understand something they've said. When I asked him how that makes him feel, he reported that it makes him feel "like a failure, bad, and ashamed." Hearing impairment doesn't have to be a disability if you're living in a community where hearing isn't highly valued and expected. But when the norm is rapid-fire speaking and you can't tune in, it can feel extremely isolating.

Similarly, ADHD wouldn't have to disable us if we could surround ourselves with a curvilinear culture – if we could be in settings where our hyper-attuned state could help us spot danger and save people's lives, or our daydreaming could be given free reign and we could do all the big-picture thinking. But in the neurotypical world, people get frustrated with us everyday. They get mad at us, and we get mad at ourselves, because we drop the ball or forget a meeting. We feel ashamed.

In a way, it's even worse that it's an invisible disability. Because we have nothing external to signal our differences, it doesn't occur to people to offer us any sort of accommodation or benefit of the doubt. We suffer in a prison of our own anxiety as a result. For your neurotypical friends who want to try to understand what that's like, I offer an extended metaphor of this invisible disability:

A Walk in My Shoes

My partner, Ben, and I dressed in our finest to go to the most expensive restaurant in our small town. It's not just a restaurant, it's an adventure of five courses, each paired with a wine and made right in front of the guests while one of the chefs talks about how they are making it and their philosophy on food. At the appointed time for this entertaining dinner theatre, the guests are brought into a room with long tables lined up one behind another on risers facing an open, stainless-steel kitchen at the front of the room. A pianist is playing lively tunes, and people are all dressed up. The guests are shown to their places and given the opportunity to chat for a bit with the other couples at their table before everyone is seated to watch the chefs begin to cook.

I wore a lovely pink dress, and I paired it with silver wedge sandals with sparkly silver straps. Before the event, we were, of course, rushed to get out of the house (time management issues), and I only put on my shoes just as we were heading out the door. That was why I didn't realize until we had parked and we were walking from the car to the restaurant that my shoes were beginning to come apart. As I walked, the straps loosed themselves one by one from their moorings even as the footbed began to peel away from the wedge sole. By the time we reached the restaurant, I had to shuffle through the door, my painted toes grasping desperately at the sandals to keep myself perched on top of them.

We had only a few minutes in the lobby area before we were supposed to be seated, so I asked for some tape and headed to the restroom with my beautiful clothes, my beautiful silver shoes, and a tape dispenser. There at the restroom sink I took off my shoes and wrapped them around and around with clear scotch tape. I taped the straps to the footbed, the footbed to the wedge, and my feet to the footbed. I artificially and not too artfully created all the connectors my sandals needed in order to function on my feet and support me. I returned to the lobby and handed back the almost empty tape dispenser to the host. The doors to the kitchen-theatre opened and we were all led in. I sat down as quickly as I could and tucked my feet under the table. It was a lovely dinner, and we had great camaraderie with the guests on either side of us. Nobody else but Ben knew that my sandals were held together with tape.

Nonetheless, I was aware the entire evening of the tenuous connection between my feet and my shoes. I was worried people would look down and notice all the scotch tape on my feet that contrasted with my fancy outfit and carefully painted toes. I worried that I'd have to leave to use the restroom, and as I stepped delicately down one of the risers, one or both of my sandals would bust apart and I'd tumble to the ground in front of everyone. Everybody else had shoes that allowed them to walk with no problems; I had to be so much more careful. I was well aware that time was ticking on how long I'd be able to keep up appearances.

With an ADHD nervous system, we may look like we walk and talk the same as everyone else, but we don't. ADHD makes it harder for us to function in basic ways that other people take for granted. And if we're trying to fit in with a culture that highly prizes executive functioning skills, we're

going to feel awkward sometimes, and we're going to need tape. Maybe that tape is coping strategies like finding a buddy at work to help us remember or follow through on important details, or keeping a calendar and setting alarms for things we must get done, or setting up reward systems for ourselves, or taking stimulant medication, or working with an ADHD coach.

We need systems in place to help us set goals and succeed at them. And we need supportive people around us who give us the benefit of the doubt when they see us trying and who are willing to give some allowances for our different skill sets. Any of you neurotypical folks out there who want to try walking in my shoes for a few blocks, feel free. They may look just like yours, but keeping up appearances isn't so easy when at any moment a strap could come loose and you could go plummeting into a ditch. You see how many gifts you can deliver when you can't keep your shoes on your feet.

By now, I'm sure you can see how this experience would lead to some major dissatisfaction with our shoes. Since they can't be returned, we'll have to work with what we've got and learn to appreciate our shoes for their other components. As we begin to be able to pinpoint and name our areas of weakness, we can start finding ways to address them so we can actually flourish in our strengths. We can stop thinking of our issues as "inadequacies," and we can stop allowing them to define us. And maybe we can start letting go of the idea that blending in should be our main goal. Maybe we are meant to stand out, to model a playful spirit, openness, willingness to put ourselves out there, enthusiasm, and intensity that's missing in so many everyday social interactions.

What would life be like if we used all the resources available to us to counteract our difficulties, including delegating tasks we're not good at and reaching out to ask for help when we need it? What if we stopped berating ourselves for all the things we never get to and instead allowed our

ADHD issues to open up opportunities for unusual, interesting, and gratifying experiences we otherwise never would have had? That's what happened for me and my son when I conquered my fears and arranged a last-minute trip for us to New York City.

Every year, right around March, I begin to anticipate Summer vacation, every teacher and student's dream. I think about the eight glorious weeks of unstructured time in which I will need to read summer reading books and plan how to teach them, entertain and spend quality time with my son, take trips, accomplish all the house projects and other things I can't get done during the school year, organize my files, create class content, hang out with friends, fit in some part-time work, and binge on sleeping, eating, and peeing. (Teachers will understand that last one very well). I tell myself I'm going to plan ahead, lay it all out, and this time I'm really going to make the very most of my summer. Yet every year, sometime in the middle of July, as I'm hurtling through a wet tube at my local water park, I realize I never got around to laying out plans and now my summer is rushing by at top speed while I flail about on my back going down a water slide like a dead bug being flushed down a drain.

I've experienced it enough that I know what's going to happen. Unfortunately, I seem to be powerless to stop it. Around July 20th, I take up the lament: "Oh how I wish I'd planned a real vacation!" "How I wish I'd made my child do some academic work!" "How I wish I'd visited more friends!" "How I wish I'd actually started my summer reading work!" "I could have done MORE!" Many of us with ADHD live in a perpetual state of dissatisfaction with our lives because we can't seem to set goals and reach them. As a result, we also experience FOMO (fear of missing out) every time we hear about other people's fabulous plans for their family vacations, or for heading to the mountains for the weekend, or having tickets to a beer festival, or whatever. We are driven as if by a motor to make things happen, yet we can't seem to make things happen. More often than not, things just happen *to* us.

Last summer, after reading the book *The Tapper Twins Tear Up New York* with my son Leo at bedtime one night, I felt sad. In the book, the Tapper twins, who go to a public middle school in New York, participate in a scavenger hunt contest that takes them all over the city. The cumulative list adds up to such a quintessential New York experience, but Leo couldn't appreciate it the way I did because he had never been there. Leo had plenty of impressions of New York gleaned from TV shows and other books he'd read. But when I asked him to describe what he thought New York City was like, he told me it was dirty, there were lots of homeless people, and it was crowded. Also, "The rich people live high up in condos." After he went to bed that night, I lamented how I could have done more to give him a better impression of New York. In all our travels, his dad and I had never taken him there.

I wanted to show him that New York City was beautiful, not just from the high up, fancy places, but from the ground. It was beautiful in its heterogeneity, in its embrace of so many different kinds of folks. New Yorkers weren't put off by eccentricity. It flourished in New York art and culture, on the subways, and in the middle of the sidewalk. Contrary to the stereotypes, New Yorkers put themselves out there and helped each other. Sure, there were rich people and poor people, but it was a lot more jumbled up. It suited my non-linear ADHD brain.

I wanted to show Leo all of this, but the problem was that I didn't know how to get past my challenges with directions, time management, and planning. I couldn't really think far enough ahead into the future to get a vacation on the schedule. Ugh, all those steps: having to research and choose transportation and accommodations, deciding on an agenda, etc. Plus, what if I made commitments and put down deposits and bought tickets and then something came up? I could, however, look as far ahead as the upcoming weekend two days away.

After I put Leo to bed that night, I checked the calendar. We didn't have any plans for the coming weekend. Hmm. I definitely couldn't drive to New York considering how easily I lose track of where I am. A flight was too expensive, and so was the Amtrak. But I'd heard people talk about a bus that went straight to Chinatown and only cost $40. I texted my friend Hadley who lived in New Jersey, just across the river from Manhattan, and I asked if we could stay with her family that weekend. Surprisingly, despite my last-minute request, she said yes. Then I went online and I booked two bus tickets to Chinatown for two days later.

Boy was Leo surprised when I told him we had a day to pack and then we had a bus to catch the next day. I took his book and photocopied the scavenger hunt page. Then I began marking the list of things I thought we could get:

- bookmark from The Strand Bookstore (Greenwich Village) – 3 points
- photo of Wall Street Charging Bull statue (Financial District) – 3 pts.
- photo of Imagine mosaic in Strawberry Fields (Central Park) – 3 pts.
- Playbill from a Broadway musical (Times Square) – 5 pts
- photo of Statue of Liberty taken from deck of Staten island ferry (Hudson River) – 10 pts
- bamboo back scratcher from Ting's (Chinatown) – 3 pts[53]

Leo thought going to New York City on a whim to recreate a scavenger hunt from a fictional children's book was crazy. I thought it was a brilliant idea. I would use the scavenger hunt in the book to help me structure our trip. Instead of getting overwhelmed by all the possible options for what to do in New York City, I had a built-in agenda. I promised him that after we hit 20 points, we would buy ourselves ice cream from a street cart. This seemed to pacify him.

That Saturday, after an eight hour bus ride where I had read a good bit of my summer reading book and Leo had played an alarming amount of video games, our bus pulled up

---

[53] Rodkey, Geoff. The Tapper Twins Tear up New York. Little, Brown. 2016.

to the curb outside a restaurant window with dead chickens hanging in it. Leo's first trip to New York City had begun. In my pocket was the photocopied page of the scavenger hunt from *The Tapper Twins Tear up New York* that had motivated this whole trip. We found ourselves a bamboo back scratcher then made our way to Penn Station to take the train to New Jersey to spend the night with Hadley and her family. I was excited to begin our adventures early the next morning to the Statue of Liberty.

The next morning, my dear neurotypical friend Hadley sent us on our way with water and snacks and directions. We took a train, walked some, took another train. Despite Hadley's directions, I still had to ask a lot of people which way to go. A LOT. As a result, we met some lovely folks, including a nice man on the train who shared with us the secret to a happy marriage (unfortunately, I forget what it was). When we got off the last train, I got confused about which direction to walk, but we quickly found a family heading to the ferry dock and followed them.

As we walked under a bridge and across a park, we had a nice conversation with the parents and their two children about their trip up the East coast in their RV. With their help, we made it to the ferry and purchased our tickets to Ellis Island. Though the Statue of Liberty requires tickets months in advance to go inside of it, we enjoyed ourselves riding the ferry and taking pictures. A mom and her two boys on the ferry told us about the fun things they'd been doing in New York and made some recommendations.

After seeing the Ellis Island Immigration Museum and the Statue of Liberty on Liberty Island, we rode the ferry to Battery Park at the tip of Manhattan. Leo had fun playing in a fountain, and from there I used Google maps on my phone to walk us to the financial district where we found the Charging Bull statue. I got a picture of Leo standing next to the little bronze girl in front of the bull. Then we walked back to Ground Zero and the 9/11 Memorial.

By this point I was feeling pretty proud of myself for my navigational skills, despite my terrible sense of direction, and for all the things we'd accomplished seeing that day. I was solely responsible for this fun experience Leo and I were having together. We got to the 9/11 Memorial, and I began taking pictures of one of the sobering pits of dark water that reflects the absence of the original twin towers. At some point, my iPhone notified me that the battery was low and it was switching to "low power" mode. I ignored it and continued taking pictures and discussing the memorial with Leo. Just as we were feeling tired and were thinking about heading back to Hadley's house, my iPhone shut down and wouldn't turn on again.

Suddenly, the worlds of "I didn't see it coming" and "How'd that happen?" collided and became "We are seriously screwed." It wasn't until my iPhone shut down that I realized the ramifications of having Hadley's address and phone number only in my phone. I had no idea where she lived other than a particular train station stop in New Jersey. I also had no map, so I had no idea where to find a train station. I also had no actual cash because I hadn't made time to get any before we

got on the bus to New York. My mind started racing with ways to solve our problem. I came up with two possible options: #1: We ask for directions to the Path train and get as far as the New Jersey station. Then we find a phone book and look up Hadley's address and take a cab there. #2: We scrounge up a piece of cardboard and a pen and write "Hungry, Homeless, Short-Sighted, Time-Blind. Please Help."
When I presented these options to Leo, he flipped out.

When you have ADHD, you're always depending on the kindness of strangers. I asked a stranger to direct us to a train station, and we were pointed towards an architecturally impressive white building just across the way. The odd structure looked like the skeleton of a bird's wings that were attempting to soar despite one wing being broken. I knew nothing about the massive white Oculus, what was inside, or what it was meant to represent. I would have Googled it, but, well, dead phone and all. I found out later that everybody has their own ideas for what the building looks like. For me, it symbolized poor Icarus from the Greek myth and my own struggles to stay aloft even as my ADHD hampers my progress.

I could have given in to feelings of shame and hopelessness. I could have told myself that I'm a terrible mother and I don't deserve to take my son on a vacation because I can't handle the basic functions of being an adult. Instead, I chose to see it as an adventure and a challenge to both of us to use our wits to get out of this predicament. I refused to let it break me. I stretched my one good wing as far as I could. I had to play to my strengths.

Leo and I entered the building and discovered a massive shopping mall inside. While I was asking a security guard directions to the trains, Leo discovered a Mac store and asked me if he could go take a look around. When I joined him, he was playing games on an iPhone. Leo takes after his dad in his interest in all things Mac, and so I indulged him for a few minutes while he played. I stood there watching him, surrounded by tables of gleaming new phones all set on power stations, when suddenly I yelled "Leo, you're a genius!"

Leo looked up from a phone: "What? Why?" he asked I took out my dead phone, took off the case, and secured it on a power dock. It came to life. Leo and I high-fived. Funny that when I was going over my options for how to get us back to Hadley's, it hadn't occurred to me to try finding a way to charge my phone. (See what I mean about how our problem-solving executive functions get seriously diminished when we're caught up in our reactions to a stimulus, aka the slight panic of being stranded in Manhattan)? 45 minutes later, we had enough juice to access Hadley's information, send a few texts, and make it back to Jersey where her husband picked us up at the station. Only later did I find out from Hadley's husband that New York City is sprinkled with public charging stations. Gee, why didn't somebody tell me that before? Well, no matter. We had met some lovely people and taken some interesting turns. I took out the scavenger hunt list – we already had 16 points!

I know that because of my ADHD I'm probably never going to win a real scavenger hunt. That kind of competition is for people who mow the lawn in straight lines and plan fabulous trips. But I don't have to sit it out, either. I can tape up my shoes and get out there, using my resources and my creativity to discover things along the way that will often be far more interesting than simply traveling from point A to point B.

15

The Inefficient Internal Motor Meets the Best Intentions

A major theme of this book is the lack of control caused by ADHD. In a lot of ways, unfortunately, we are tragic heroes guided by our own fundamental flaws towards a tragic fate we are doomed to fulfill. Or, at least that's a highly likely outcome if we don't recognize and learn to manage our weaknesses and play to our strengths. We really are lucky that we're so creative. It often allows us to head off disaster even when we're headed straight for it. Our creativity allows us to find ways to work with the out-of-control feeling we often have. Since ADHD is a fundamental problem with self-regulation, we will always be coping with an inefficient and faulty motor that doesn't reliably take us where we'd like to go. Our lives are governed by "either/or." Either we are on or off, motivated or shut down, over or under-stimulated. If our shoes are the motor that moves us forward, either they hamper us by being inadequate and coming apart, or they are glued to our feet, spinning us in pointless circles with no goal in sight.

The latter problem brings us to another story about shoes, the old Russian folk tale "The Red Shoes." In this story with various permutations, the red shoes are exquisitely made shoes that are given as a gift to their wearer. They are beautiful and appealing, but they are also cursed shoes that force their wearer to dance and dance and push her to utter exhaustion. Once they are on her feet, the little orphan girl (or the ballerina, depending on which version of the story we're telling) can't get them off. They drive her mercilessly onward, despite her desperate attempts to stop dancing. They make their wearer cover the same ground over and over and there is no escape. They determine her fate, and she has no control. Eventually, they lead to her death or destruction.

For those of us with our restless internal motor stuck on full throttle, we can identify with the relentless dance and the inability to control where our feet take us. We often go to bed utterly exhausted without having produced much in the way of accomplishments. We ADHD-ers are often very busy *doing* but surprisingly lacking in the *getting things done* part, especially when we don't have a rigid daily structure. Again, this is because our brains don't move in linear fashion. A lot of creativity can happen when we move in all directions at once, but also a lot of chaos and exhaustion can ensue.

We may desperately wish sometimes that we could take off the red shoes and stop the spinning and spinning. When it comes to accomplishing tasks and meeting goals, we may spin all day in every direction, but often the end result is no closer to attainment. Somehow there's just "one more thing" that needs to happen before the actual thing can happen, and that "one more thing" and "one more thing" just seem to go on forever.

Thankfully, ADHD coaching, cognitive behavioral therapy or dialectical behavior therapy, as well as medication, can often be valuable tools to help us overcome some of our inefficiencies and to gain some handle on our lives. Once that happens, it frees us up to make some meaning out of our bombardment of daydreams, ideas, and good intentions, and to reach a potential we may never have thought possible. Is it really asking too much that we be capable of creating our own beautiful dance?

I never know exactly what will happen when vacations pull my daily structure and routines out from under me. My experience last winter break was most certainly a dance of the red shoes as my best intentions for accomplishing fairly simple organizing tasks put me on a crash course with chaos. My restless internal motor (The "H" in ADHD) sent me every which way without giving me a moment's peace.

It all began the day after Christmas when I was putting away the Christmas bags and tissue paper. In the basement, the large plastic bin I was using to store everything had been rifled through by various family members looking for gift bags to wrap Christmas presents. There were gift bags, tissue paper, and scraps of wrapping paper sticking out everywhere. I sat on the floor and began pulling things out of the bin so I could lay everything flat again. I stacked the bags together by size on the floor and separated them from the tissue and wrapping papers that I smoothed into neat stacks as well.

As I kept pulling things out, I also discovered Halloween gift bags, baby shower gift bags, Valentine's gift bags, and birthday gift bags all mixed in with the Christmas stuff. I also found an old (and I mean OLD) Ghirardelli chocolate square wrapped in sparkly green and white foil. It was labeled "chocolate peppermint brownie" which was so compelling to me that, after checking for nibble marks from a mouse, I am ashamed to say I went ahead and ate it. It was surprisingly good. Then I buckled down and decided "I'm gonna organize this bin!" All around me, in a big circle, I created piles of gift bags differentiated by size and holiday. I even separated the tissue paper into spring colors, Valentine's colors, Halloween colors, and Christmas colors. Then I stood up, surveyed my perfect circle of stacks, and went upstairs for lunch.

When my restless feet took me back downstairs a couple of hours later and I rediscovered my piles of bags (out of sight, out of mind), it occurred to me that I could use another bin to make finding gift bags easier. I had just the perfect sized bin in mind, but it was full of baby clothes from over a decade ago. I pulled it down off the wire rack where it was stored and began going through the clothes, holding up each item and remembering when Leo had worn the wee hand-knitted sweaters and the green velour outfit with lions on it. I remembered that "I was gonna" deal with these clothes years ago. Today would be the day. All the clothes smelled musty, so I began separating them into piles for the wash. I put my first load of baby clothes into the washer, and then I went back into the room with the gift bags, wielding my new, now empty, perfect-sized bin.

I began the gratifying process of packing each bin with seasonal bags and tissue papers. When I was done, I carried the bins to the closet and congratulated myself on a project completed. On my way back to the laundry room, I saw the wooden toddler chair that had been sitting in the storage room for ages. "I was gonna" sell that. I had written a note on the whiteboard months ago telling myself to sell it. Flush with my victory on the last project, I took the chair into a well-lit room to take some pictures and get it listed on Facebook. That's when I remembered there was some hardware that went with the chair that I was pretty sure was in the upstairs hall closet.

My frenetic dance continued as upstairs I went to locate the missing hardware. I opened the hall closet. A tape measure, a couple of screws, and a roll of duct tape fell out onto my foot. I'd been telling myself for the longest time that "I was gonna" organize that closet. There were four shelves covered in games, lightbulbs, candles, cookbooks, small bins of hardware, tool boxes, placemats and napkins. You couldn't find anything in there! I just needed to do "one more thing" and reorganize all this stuff in order to find that hardware I was looking for. What better time to organize the hall closet than during winter break? I began pulling out everything one shelf at a time and stacking it all along the floor of the hallway.

I need to digress for a moment into another analogy. Leo has always loved Bert and Ernie from Sesame Street. I think those two loveable muppets are a great way to illustrate the pitfalls of a linear thinker (Bert) living with a non linear-thinker (Ernie). In one famous episode, Bert is about to take a bath, but Ernie tells him that he needs to add something to the bathtub to make it more pleasant. He offers his rubber duckie, and Bert thanks him. Bert is just about to get into the tubbie when Ernie says "Wait Bert, you just need one more thing…" He gets Bert a nice glass of water to take into the tub. Bert is again about to get in when Ernie tells him "you just need one more thing," goes to the kitchen and comes back with a large submarine sandwich. He keeps adding "one more thing" until the bathtub is completely filled with items, including a piano and finally an elephant. Bert exclaims in exasperation that now he can't even take a bath because the tub is too full of all those things.

It was like that with my trying to get the hardware back downstairs to the toddler chair. I was so busy pulling things out to find the hardware that I barely had room to move in the hallway anymore. An hour later, the hallway was choked with tottering stacks of cookbooks that I rarely used, placemats, tablecloths, and towels, and tools everywhere, as well as various old cat items that I no longer needed. Thankfully, I did manage to find the black metal bar with the two screws attached to it that I needed for the toddler chair. Victory! But it didn't seem right to take it downstairs before I cleaned up my huge mess upstairs.

I tried to put the nice, neat stacks of placemats and dish towels back onto a now empty shelf, but it overhung the narrow shelf in a way I didn't like. Then I decided that a better place for the placemats and towels would be in the kitchen cabinet. After all, that would put the placemats closer to the dining room table and the towels closer to the kitchen sink. Genius idea. There was a bunch of junk in one of the kitchen cabinets and "I was gonna" clean it out anyway, so I'd just do "one more thing…"

29 minutes later…

… and that's how another stack of cookbooks, old dishes, teapots, and pots ended up on top of the kitchen counter. I'm surprised I didn't go ahead and put a piano and an elephant there as well.

By this point I was craving a chocolate croissant. It was 8pm and all day "I was gonna" go to the grocery store for milk. I put the placemats in the bottom kitchen cabinet, felt gratified that they fit well there, put on my coat, and left.

The next morning I navigated my way down the hallway to the kitchen past haphazard stacks of cookbooks, papers, boxes of hardware, cat toys, and partially evaporated bubble wands. Sitting at the dining room table, croissant in hand, a feeling of paralysis came over me as I considered the stuff all over the floor and counters I still didn't know what to do with. That's when I decided to finish listing the toddler chair for sale on Facebook. However, before I got that done, an ad popped up for a food delivery service.

The food company buys ugly, cast off fruits and vegetables from farms and grocery stores. They seek out the misfits and the rejects, the misshapen and the blemished, and instead of wasting this perfectly good food, they then sell it for a fair price. They give fresh fruits and veggies a chance even though they don't look just like the rest of their kind. I can totally get behind that. So I signed up. After all, if I expect people to give me the benefit of the doubt for my imperfections, I should put my money where my mouth is, right?

And this is what happens when I don't have my usual daily structure to follow. My body moves like my mind: up and down the stairs, in and out of closets, outside and back inside, never at rest, merely perching until the next thought sends me down the hall, up a ladder (that happened, too. I left that out), deep inside a cabinet, round and round from room to room, pulling out more and more things, making more and more lists and promises and plans…Just "one more thing" and "one more thing" until inevitably I become overwhelmed by a teetering stack of things in the hallway/on the counter/in the basement and then abandon it all and succumb to whatever interests me in the moment.

If only I could experience the satisfaction of controlling just one small outcome. Maybe I could make the junk drawer pretty, or I could actually sell that chair. But no, the "red shoes" of ADHD propel me in endless spinning. What is the biological reason for this happening? It seems to be in the timing of brain development. According to Dr. Barkley, Savior of the Scattered, a National Institute of Mental Health study showed that "the primary motor system of the brain—the part that gives rise to various and small motor movements—appears to mature too early in those with ADHD." Whereas, the higher-level brain center that controls our impulses and organizes us towards future goals develops late.[54] In other words, it's a restless internal motor with less-than-robust brakes for the rest of our lives.

The best I can do to slow down is to draw a nice, warm bath and settle in among the elephants and the pianos. Finally, my internal motor is submerged. And for a little while, at least, there's some calm amidst the chaos.

---

[54] *Taking Charge of Adult ADHD* Pg. 59

16

Problems with Prioritizing
and Follow-Through

My "dance of the red shoes" is actually more a "dance of the random piles." I feel like my whole life has been about the piles. I can stack things till the end of time, but I can't seem to get them sorted individually and put away. Paperwork is the worst. When it's something I know I should deal with – a stack of mail, a bill, a company I need to call, a receipt I might need, a magazine I want to read, a retirement account statement – I don't want to put it out of sight because then I'll never get to it. So, I make little stacks all over the kitchen counter. Sometimes, when I've been feeling fancy, I've used a system of stacked and labeled trays, but the piles just grow within them and the paperwork ends up spilling out everywhere. Once the piles get too big, I seem to be incapable of touching them. The potential sensory overload is so acute that I literally can't make myself deal with them.

Casey used to get tired of my kitchen counter piles, so periodically he'd stack them all together and deposit them into my home office. When I went into my office to find those large stacks of paperwork sitting on the floor, I felt paralyzed. How could he not understand what happened to me when he put all my little stacks together? I was doomed to repeat the cycle of going through the same paperwork over and over, getting it into manageable piles, and then not being able to fully get rid of it, only to find that the piles had been thrown together again. I would never get out from under them.

I imagine that touching one of those immense piles would be like going outside and taking the cover off my grill. Several months ago, a squirrel ate a hole in the grill cover and made his home inside it. I've been afraid to use my grill since then, for fear that when I lift off the cover the squirrel will come flying out and attack me. There is the same anxious fear in my body when it comes to pulling apart those piles. I'm just bracing for an attack of guilt (for finding out I missed an important deadline on something), or an attack of indecision (for having to decide what to do with stuff), or an attack of claustrophobia (for when I'm surrounded by my paperwork but all I want to do is escape my responsibilities and go to a festival).

Ben, on the other hand, gets me. He and I both have a system for piles. We call them our "compost bins" because we find that if we leave things in there long enough, they become irrelevant. If you let something sit long enough, the urge to keep it kind of evaporates over time, and then it's easy to get rid of. Stuff I thought was important a year ago pretty much loses most of its potency once I realize it's too late to do anything with it. It's not a great system, but it's what I have to work with: the whirling dervish dance of perpetual spinning, followed by The Stacks of Inertia.

William Carlos Williams once wrote a poem titled "This is Just to Say." It appears to be a simple letter, perhaps to his wife, where the narrator admits to eating the plums that the other person was probably planning to eat. It's a letter of apology but also a confession of guilty pleasure:

This is Just to Say
By William Carlos Williams

I have eaten
the plums
that were in
the icebox

and which
you were probably
saving
for breakfast

Forgive me
they were delicious
so sweet
and so cold

There's an unspoken subtext, an expectation that the other person knows the narrator intimately enough, knows the relationship with fresh plums intimately enough to understand. It's as if the narrator is saying "Of course you understand. I simply couldn't help myself. They were calling to me. Anyone would have done the same in my place. One of us was going to get something delightful out of eating those plums, and it just so happened to be me."

What I love about the poem is that the narrator seems quite certain he will be forgiven, that the other person will understand. He didn't eat those plums to be mean or selfish. It wasn't a vindictive act. It was an act of pure in-the-moment ecstasy. He desires to share with his mate what that felt like, not to make the other feel bad, but because he knows that on some level his mate will identify with that joy and be happy for him.

My ex husband did not identify with my stimulation-seeking moments when I needed to escape the tedium of a project or chore that I had no capacity to separate into clear steps and accomplish. He saw it as bizarre, irresponsible behavior, though he did joke about it because I did it so often. One of my main weaknesses has always been festivals. I could have a whole Saturday lined up of things that I'd promised to take care of--paperwork, projects, grocery shopping--but if I found out there was a festival happening--apple festivals, oyster festivals, art festivals, music festivals, strawberry festivals--I'd drop everything and head out to be part of the celebratory feeling. Casey tolerated this behavior, but he didn't feel my joy, my relief at turning towards the high-interest stimulation and avoiding the boring tasks. I wrote this poem to the ideal mate who would truly understand how priorities work for me:

This is Just to Say
by Vanessa Jones

I have neglected
again
to find something
for dinner

which probably
doesn't surprise you
since I never plan,
anyway.

Forgive me.
There was a festival
And I
was the May Queen.

My loyalties are to whatever high-interest stimulation I can get in the moment, not to what needs to happen or to what will be. Those trifling matters simply drag one down and keep one from the extraordinary. After all, if you weigh "making dinner" against becoming the May Queen, any person like me would clearly be able to see the payoff to living life for the fun of it.

17

The ADHD Organizational System

Thank goodness for the backs of envelopes. That's where everyone writes down important information, right? As far as I'm concerned, this is what the mail is for, to provide backs of envelopes sitting on the counter ready to receive important phone numbers, names of contractors, to do lists, directions to places, shopping lists, and the exact amount needed when I write that check to refinance my mortgage.

I grab the nearest scrap of paper and scribble sideways in the margins with an old mini golf pencil when I'm driving and I hear something on a podcast that I want to remember. My car is littered with receipts, magazine subscription inserts, paper napkins, and junk mail all scrawled with phone numbers, websites, useful quotations, and dates of events. I build lesson plans from scraps of paper on which I've written ideas, resources, and outlines.

I am in fact right now looking at a coupon from Chewy that I received in the mail. The only white space to write on is the rectangular address box. It's covered in my handwriting. The first bullet point says "aware and informed." I remember grabbing that coupon off the counter when Ben was saying something about relationships that I wanted to remember. I wrote down this bullet point, but sadly I didn't have room to write down any more context than that.

Of course, I also write notes in my phone (running lists in no particular order), make voice memos to myself (without titling them. They just say "Recording 24," "Recording 25," etc.), and keep a list of to-do's on my white board on my wall. In addition, I have two notebooks and two legal pads and a second notes app on my phone, all for documenting things I want to remember. I've tried scheduling reminders of tasks in my phone and putting things I want to get done on my calendar at a certain date and time, but scraps of paper still feel the most natural to me as an organizational method. I seem to be able to associate each scrap of paper --its size, colors, texture, fonts, shape, thickness--with whatever important thing I wrote on it. That makes it easier to find later--as long as someone else in the household doesn't decide it's time to get rid of all my "trash."

More often than not, however, I don't actually use what I've written on my scraps of paper. Rather, they become part of the general background of clutter in my life. A year or so ago, I took a bunch of notes at a "nonviolent communication" workshop I went to. I wrote my notes in the margins and between the printed lines on the worksheets we were given. I was gonna type up the notes and make a nice digital folder to put them in, but instead the pages with my notes resided on the couch for awhile, then on the floor next to the couch, then on a shelf, then on the dining room table, then back on the floor. Over the course of several months, the dog walked all over them, tearing and wrinkling the pages, water spilled on them, and somebody stepped on them with a dirty shoe (talk about violent)! In the end I never did type up those notes, but I did stuff the wrinkled, torn, and dirty pages into a file in my desk drawer.

"Scrap of paper" research is my particular specialty. We ADHD-ers are very good at researching things we want to know more about. We can spend hours researching the pros and cons of dish drainers if that's what suddenly seems important to us. We find decision-making stressful, and often our research is aimed at helping us feel better equipped to make decisions big and small – which car to buy, where to go on vacation, what toothpaste would be best, whether to get a memory foam pillow or a regular foam pillow or one stuffed with down. One problem for many of us, though, is that our anxiety about getting it "wrong" causes us to hyperfocus on every possible aspect of the topic at hand – spending hours learning about bicycle pumps, for example – without knowing when to stop.

One of two things tends to happen to get us to finally make a decision. Either an external cue such as a deadline forces us to abandon the research and take action, or we may simply tire of the research and after all that agonizing pick something more or less at random just to be done with it. A third path is that something else grabs our attention, and we forget about the topic entirely.

My research tends to take me an inordinately long amount of time because I write incomplete information on nearby scraps of paper and then don't actually have what I need to make an informed decision. For example, when I was researching cabinet pulls for the kitchen, I went through hundreds of images of cabinet pulls and wrote down the colors and styles I liked best. However, when I was finally ready to make a decision, I couldn't go back and find any of the pulls I'd written down because I didn't know which one of four different websites I'd found them on or what style number to put into the search bar. What seemed like the most pertinent information at the time actually wasn't what I needed to be able to complete the purchase. So, after combing back through Etsy to find one of my top choices again, I just went ahead and bought those pulls to avoid the hassle of having to find the others all over again.

Many ADHD-ers report going through the motions of careful and thorough research and agonizing inner debate over a decision, only to find that when confronted with the moment of decision-making, an almost tranquil impulsivity takes over and much of what we've learned goes out the window. It's a quick escape from information overload and the tedium of details.

This interesting "thorough/impulsive" dichotomy may well explain how you can have all the information in the world about roofing companies that you wrote on a scrap of paper, yet when your husband reminds you to schedule the roofing right before you go on vacation, you can't find that scrap of paper. So in the end you call the first company you find online, causing you to end up with roofers who let your attic flood while you were away because they neglected to tarp the roof properly when a rainstorm came through.

Or perhaps you want to buy a new car and you've narrowed it down to the kind of car you want and made appointments for test-drives at several dealerships. But then you just go ahead and buy the first one you try (an older model with sensor problems) because you're on your way to the airport and you're running late and you already sold your old car during a snowstorm two days ago, so you'll need a car when you get back from your trip. (Both of these stories, by the way, are completely true).

My most critical scraps of paper are those on which I've written usernames and passwords for all the accounts to which I'm forced to register. It seems like every time I try to use my computer for anything, I have to make an account. Do I want to see my child's grades? Make a username and password. Want to read an online article? Make a username and password. Want to make animated commercials with your students? Want to join the frequent-pizza club? Want to have access to the Playstation? It goes on and on. I have hundreds of usernames and passwords, and I have NO IDEA what most of them are. I tried saving all my usernames and passwords in a password management service, but for some reason it never autofills when I need it to, and it doesn't work on my phone most of the time. So, I went back to my trusty scraps of paper, and as long as I'm home to find them in my piles, I have what I need.

Most ADHD-ers live in a perpetual world of clutter, especially on our desks. Paperwork and digital clutter is the bane of our existence. We just cannot effectively prioritize, follow-through, and throw away. But at least when the paper clutter gets too extreme, I can tell because I have piles that I can see and touch. Digital clutter, such as email messages, is a whole other problem. I have three email accounts for different parts of my life. In the account I've had the longest, I have over one million bold messages in my inbox. 166, 917 of those are unread. As the unread and spam messages piled up, I couldn't really "feel" how bad it was getting until it was completely out of control.

Now, my only recourse is probably going to be to ditch the account altogether and start over. Or, I could just avoid looking at it, ever. My digital clutter weighs on me in a vague, distant way. I seem to have no resources to get out from under it. My downloads folder is so full, my computer is running slower. My computer desktop screen looks like it's been decoupaged with thumbnail images of documents. My Google Drive is a mess of random materials with no organizing folders.

I've paid people a couple of times to help me organize my home and office. It worked, for a little while. But things slowly started to get out of hand until eventually I was back where I started. I've even joined decluttering webinars and written notes on how to declutter (on scraps of paper, of course), but it just doesn't stick. The thing about ADHD is that we can't find much success using an approach handed to us by a linear thinker. We might be able to understand the method intellectually, but it doesn't compute in a deeper, visceral way.

I'm going to guess that the inventor of Post-it notes had ADHD because Post-its are such perfect little scraps of paper with fun colors, to boot. Maybe instead of feeling bad about my organizational system, I should just find a way to capitalize on it.

18

An ADHD Approach to Money-Management

Speaking of capitalizing, we ADHD-ers have an interesting relationship with money. We are such creative thinkers that some of us have found ways to make a lot of money with inventions, business ventures, and spotting opportunities that others don't see. However, we have working memory issues, so the amount of money we have and the amount of money we've spent don't always represent very accurately in our mind's eye.

Some of us spend money freely, our impulsivity getting the best of us even when we don't really have the money to support it. Some of us do the exact opposite, tightly controlling every expenditure like our lives depend on it because we fear it will slip through our fingers and we'll be left with nothing. Some of us vacillate between these two extremes--sometimes being cheapskates, and sometimes spending lavishly, with no real idea what the trigger will be to turn us into either Scrooge or an Emperor. Many of us report that thinking about our finances fills us with dread. It's as though our money is behind a dirty glass window, and it's hard to make out what's what through the smudges and the bird poop. Plus, it keeps changing based on our spending habits and what we bring in from month to month. Who can keep track of all that?

A few of us are actually pretty good at handling the finances, perhaps because our anxiety about the ability to maintain a comfortable lifestyle or a roof over our heads motivates us to stay on track. For the rest of us, our non-ADHD partners often end up taking over the finances. Having ADHD costs us, and other people, money. Our partners don't need their credit ruined because we forgot to pay the bills. We also cost our families money when we lose or quit our jobs because we can't get along with people at work or we can't make ourselves fulfill certain work duties. I know more than one person who impulsively quit work one day and then came home and announced it to their spouse.

Our impulsivity and need for stimulation make us particularly susceptible to a "good deal" or an "exciting" product. Though I try to stay strong, I have a tendency to get taken in by telemarketers offering me all-inclusive cruises and resort stays for a fraction of the cost if I'm willing to "buy now." These vacation packages generally don't expire for two to three years. It's the perfect scam to take advantage of an ADHD-er with a credit card in their pocket and a short memory. The salesperson describes the tropical resort package, says they'll throw in a rental car, tells me they'll give it all to me at cost, and I get a feel-good hit of dopamine as I anticipate the fun I'll have and the money I'll save. Next thing I know, I'm enduring an interminable time-share presentation in Mexico, or I'm sitting in my hotel room in Florida, unable to enjoy the pool and hot tub because an Orthodox Jewish community has rented out most of the space for a private event. (Hmm, why didn't they tell me that before?) Or I've lost the information they sent in the email after I agreed to the charges, and I have no record or memory of ever having purchased a vacation.

I'm also a particular sucker for expensive clothing on sale. I'll see a gorgeous designer ball gown that's 75% off, decide to try it on for fun, love how wearing it makes me feel like a princess, and then buy it even though I'll never have a place to wear it. (Though, of course, I'm sure there will be a formal event on my next discount cruise to the Bahamas). Then there was the pair of leather pants that a very expensive store in town had on its sale rack for years. They were $1200 pants, on sale for $300, but still no one was buying them. I tried to put them on in the dressing room, but the waist band wouldn't stretch enough to get them over my hips. I realized that what the pants needed was simply a hidden zipper along the side seam. Without that, no adult woman could possibly get them on.

I wrote a post-it note to the owner offering $100 for the pants and left it with the salesperson. Two weeks later, I got a call that the owner would sell them to me for what I'd proposed. I went in, purchased the pants, and got the seamstress at the store to put a zipper into them for $30. And Voila! I had a new pair of leather pants that fit me perfectly! Every time I tell this story, I get excited all over again. It was a thrill to make the discovery of how to fix the pants; it was a thrill to convince the owner to sell them to me for my price; it was a thrill to take the risk that they would fit once a zipper was in place; it was a thrill to try them on when they were all done and to have the salespeople shake their heads in wonder that finally the pants fit someone – me! Sure, I have no place to wear leather pants, and I did still end up spending $130 I hadn't planned to spend, but what a deal. That's the thing about the "But it was on sale!" mentality. It's a glass half-full approach. Instead of "Here's how much I spent," it's "Look how much I saved!"

I took an ADHD friend with me on one of my bad-idea telemarketing cruises. She had a fantastic strategy for managing money while gambling. I was on a roll playing roulette, tossing gaming chips down on whatever color or number struck my fancy, and getting rewarded with plenty of dopamine and more plastic tokens worth real money. Of course I wasn't keeping track of how much money I was winning or losing. I just kept playing with whatever was on the table. But every time I won, my friend immediately grabbed the highest value tokens out of my hand and stuffed them into the back pocket of my jeans. I was so caught up in the pace of the game that I kept forgetting those tokens were in my back pocket. When I ran out of tokens on the table, we got up to leave, and that's when my friend reminded me to check my back pocket to see what I had to cash in. I'd won $200! Now that's a friend who understands what I need.

This same strategy works great when applied to savings accounts, as well. I once had an IRA that I lost track of for 25 years! I guess it was deep in my back pocket. But boy, when I found it again, it had made some money. I do find that splitting my money up and stashing it in different places helps me not to spend it. I try to protect the money I must have for things like mortgage and insurance. If everything I had in the world was all out there on the table in one account, there's no telling what I'd end up spending it on.

Groceries and household items present another special challenge to us ADHD-ers. Ongoing necessities like these generate a constant headache in the weaker planning and prioritizing parts of our brains. Our hyperactivity (restlessness) makes it hard for us to sit still, go through recipes, and plan out menus ahead of time. We just want to get moving and get the shopping done. And even when we do some planning, we may find ourselves getting high-interest stimulation from time-consuming and difficult recipes with hard-to-find ingredients. Next thing you know, we have a beautiful list on a scrap of paper that includes small Japanese eggplants and a Thai chili oil we can't get at the neighborhood Food Lion. Instead of prioritizing eggs and milk, we go out of our way to find the special ingredients two towns over, and then we never get around to making the time-consuming recipe, and the poor Japanese eggplants rot in the fridge.

Alternatively, we go to the grocery store with no plan whatsoever, and we wander the aisles throwing anything that looks good into our carts. I guess I'm beginning to see why my ex-husband didn't seem to be appreciative when I took care of the grocery shopping. I recall him muttering something about how he couldn't ever find anything to make even though I'd just been to the store.

19

Problems "Feeling" Time

I have a child who has an impeccable sense of time. Even without a watch or a phone, he always seems to know what time it is when we are out doing things. He knows how long things will take, when we should leave for events and appointments to get there on time, and how to set schedules for himself. It drives him up the wall when I say we are just going to do one or two errands and it won't take long, and then I run into a neighbor and chat for 20 minutes and add three more errands to the list at the last minute. Or we go to a museum and I say we'll be there for two hours, and then I feel compelled to read every single wall plaque and we've missed lunch and he can't drag me away.

I respect Leo's need for time and structure, and I work hard to minimize the disruptions to his life caused by my lack of time sensitivity. He also recognizes how difficult it is for me to keep to a schedule, and he's usually pretty forgiving if my time lapses aren't too extreme. Nonetheless, he's taken to preferring to stay home alone rather than to accompany me on errands since he has more control over his own time that way. I thought perhaps that he'd like to come with me to meet a pot-bellied therapy pig that a woman wanted me to pet sit, but he told me to go ahead and just asked that I be back soon. I told Leo that I'd just be gone half an hour, since the woman with the pig lived close by, and I left him playing video games on the couch.

When I got there, the woman showed me into her living room to meet the pig. She suggested I put my purse (with my phone in it) on the shelf under the TV so the pig wouldn't get it and root through it. Then I sat on the couch and the pig jumped up and flopped over next to me. I scratched its weird little tummy while the family's dog sat at my feet looking up at me begging to be scratched, too. After that, I got a tour of the pig's playroom on the screened in porch that contained a wading pool and pig toys, and the backyard where the pig and the dog could be put out on two lines attached to a cable. The pig was very smart and could get his line untangled from the dog's without much trouble. Then I had to learn what and when to feed the pig and its many other habits and proclivities. It was all so interesting and bizarre that I totally forgot I'd promised Leo I'd be home in half an hour. It was a fully immersive pig-world experience.

Finally, the woman finished explaining to me all the nuances of her pig's day. She thanked me for coming to meet the pig, I got my purse out from under the TV, and I walked back to my car. Once I was in the car, I pulled out my phone to find my screen full of messages from Leo. I checked the time. An hour and a half had gone by! I had eight text messages from my son saying "mom, get back here" and "Srsly come on" and "It's 4:50" and "Mom!!!!!!!!!!!!!!!!!!" I scanned through those messages, immediately got a hit of adrenaline from how guilty and ashamed I felt for having lost track of time, and peeled out of the cul-de-sac fueled by worry about Leo being alone so long and the long-term trauma he would surely suffer because he didn't know what had happened to me or if I would ever return.

When I got home, I ran through the door, enveloped my child in a hug, and apologized profusely for having been gone so long and for worrying him. He pushed away, went back to his video game, and said "I wasn't worried. You just said you'd be back in half an hour." He said this as though half an hour was some kind of objective measurement that stayed the same no matter what! To me, it *felt* like only half an hour had gone by, but apparently that didn't cut it. Exact measurements of time have much more meaning for Leo, and I had defiled time itself with my lack of respect for a proper half an hour.

My mom won a national poetry contest many years ago sponsored by our local grocery store chain. I think it perfectly expresses the way time gets away from us ADHD-ers. In this poem, she only intends to be a minute at the grocery store, except that her impulsivity and susceptibility to a good sale makes it much more of an adventure:

Minute Waltz
By Ruth Jones

"I'll just run in and out," I say
"To buy one item for today.
It won't take long, I won't go far
You can wait here in the car."

I leave my husband's crooked smile
And dash straight towards the produce aisle.
A sign nearby the pears I seek
says "buy one, get one free this week."

My eyes light up, two items more,
And then I'll exit from the store.
But passing by a huge display
The cake mix is on sale today.

What's one more box? I think awhile
Then add it to the growing pile.
I see a friend whose cart displays
Several jars of mayonnaise.

"Bonus buys, coupons galore,"
she says, "and I have several more.
So here you go, just take a few."
And soon I have some mayo, too.

My watch reveals it's almost noon
We'll all be hungry very soon.
There's no bologna, home, I fear.
I'll get some deli while I'm here.

Rolls and mustard will go nice
and maybe pizza, just a slice.
Chips and pickles, slaw and cheese and
"May I have some donuts, please?"

A neighbor stops me, she's been told
The house beside us has been sold.
New folks would soon be stopping by,
I rush right back and get a pie.

Oh dear, coffee? tea? I can't think
I'll just get one of every drink.
Milk, and juice, and ginger ale
Enough that I just cannot fail.

"Would you like a yogurt pop?"
 Asks the lady, as I stop.
"I like this," says another shopper
"This is a terrific offer."

To frozen food! I don't think twice
And there I find ice-cream, half price.
"Enough," I say, "I can be tough.
I am buying no more stuff."

Flushed with success, I get in line
And check out fast; things go just fine.
Never asking where I've been,
My husband smiles and helps me in.

Once home we unpack, put away
In freezer, pantry… "what did you say?"
"Where," he says, "did you put the pear?
I cannot find it anywhere."

I throw my hands up in dismay
"I guess we're going back today"
"This time," he says with jaw set straight,
"I'll go in, you sit and wait."

As you can see, the apple doesn't fall far from the tree.
When faced with a high-stimulation activity, time completely

gets away from both me and my mom. When I was little, I thought she and I had completely different mindsets around shopping. I remember trailing my mom around the grocery store while she took forever because she had to go through her box of coupons in every aisle to see what she could save money on. She bought things purely because she had coupons for them or they were on sale, even if we didn't need them or we might have preferred a different brand. The amount of time it took her to clip coupons from the Sunday paper, organize them in her file box, and then sift through them at the grocery store just to save 20 cents or maybe even $1.00 seemed absurd to me. At a young age, I vowed to myself that I would never clip coupons.

I'm not diagnosing my mom with ADHD, but the way she describes getting caught up in the overwhelming stimulation of food, neighbors, and sales until she loses all track of time is definitely something we ADHD-ers can relate to. For my mom, coupon-clipping was probably a serviceable coping strategy to keep her impulsivity in check and to stay relatively focused. She grew up with parents who had depression-era habits around spending, and so saving money any way they could and not wasting what they had was held up as a moral victory.

I'm certain that every time she found a coupon in her box for a product we could use, she got a little boost of dopamine at the thought of the money she was saving. How much money she could save was her measure of time. As an adult with my own susceptibility to sales, I now find I'm much the same way. If there are enough sales to stimulate me, I can go for hours and hours with no break, just running on the pure thrill of the chase.

I have to hand it to my mom, though, she always managed to come up with dinners to make, every single night, without fail. Dinner was actually ready at dinnertime, too. Poor Leo suffers a bit of a jolt every time he comes back to me from Casey's house because he gets used to eating good, homemade food right around 6pm each night. At Casey's house, Leo is used to asking "What's for dinner tonight?" sometime around lunchtime and getting an answer. At our house, I just look at him and laugh. How would I know what's for dinner so far ahead of dinnertime? Ben and I have a different question that we ask each other every night when it becomes apparent that we're hungry. Just after most regular Americans have finished their dinners and are cleaning up the dishes or throwing away their takeout boxes, one of us will wander into the kitchen, start opening cabinets and say to the other "Do we have anything for dinner?" It drives Leo nuts that sometimes we don't eat until 8pm.

We also often eat our vegetables after the fact, if we get to them at all, as we can't seem to make the main meal plus a vegetable at the same time. We'll be sitting down to eat and I'll promise to make green beans when we're done, then inevitably I'll forget or I won't have the energy. If we do, by some miracle, actually manage to get a protein, a vegetable, and some other side on the table all at one time roughly around what most people consider to be the dinner hour, and it actually tastes decent, we spend the rest of the evening congratulating ourselves and eating ice cream.

Research has demonstrated clear differences between ADHD and non ADHD brains in terms of how we relate to time. People with ADHD demonstrate impairment not only in our perception of time, i.e. how long we *think* something should take or has taken, but also in time sequencing tasks and processing speed (how quickly things can be done). In other words, when asked to reproduce or to verbally estimate the duration of a stimulus, we either significantly underestimate or overestimate the duration. We also lose track of what happened first, second, third, and so on when it comes to remembering things chronologically. And finally, many of us have a slower output of both verbal and motor response to tasks that require rapid speed.[55]

We ADHD-ers don't seem to perceive time as a sequence but rather as a jumbled collection of events, emotions, and activities.[56] We may not "feel" time, but we do seem to "feel" our way through the world depending on what emotions and reactions different situations elicit from us. As I said before, I remember things based on what emotions are attached to them. As a result, my perception of time slows down or speeds up depending on my level of emotional engagement. If there's nothing to draw me in emotionally,

---

[55]Ptacek R, Weissenberger S, Braaten E, Klicperova-Baker M, Goetz M, Raboch J, Vnukova M, Stefano GB. Clinical Implications of the Perception of Time in Attention Deficit Hyperactivity Disorder (ADHD): A Review. Med Sci Monit. 2019 May 26;25:3918-3924. doi: 10.12659/MSM.914225. PMID: 31129679; PMCID: PMC6556068.
[56]Paul, Jaclyn. "How It Really Feels to Be Time-Blind with ADHD." *ADHD Homestead.net*, 11 Apr. 2018, https://adhdhomestead.net/time-blindness-feels/.

(such as no stories or pictures in a book I have to read), my attention wanders and I have a vague, disquieting sense of time passing me by while I try to force myself to stay on task. By contrast, if my feelings are stimulated, such as when I meet a therapy pig for the first time, my sense of time passing becomes shorter.

People with ADHD are very attuned to "story." We read situations and emotions. It's not that surprising, then, that while we perform poorly on time perception when it comes to neutral stimuli, research has demonstrated that we actually perform better than our neurotypical peers when it comes to perceiving time related to emotional stimuli. We also more easily interpret situational stimuli and pictures.[57] Researchers hypothesize that this is because we can default from temporal processing (where we have issues) to emotional processing (an area we've strengthened as a coping mechanism for weak executive functioning), while the control group, on the other hand, has to split their attention between temporal and emotional processes, thereby weakening both.

Despite our time weaknesses, we really do have some strengths. But unfortunately for us, the people with whom we interact often take offense, lose respect for us, and feel unloved when we can't manage our time. They feel we don't value them as much as we value whatever else we had been doing. Our intentions are good, we know this, but others question them all

---

[57] Nazari MA, Mirloo MM, Rezaei M, Sotanlou M. Emotional Stimuli facilitate time perception in children with attention-deficit/hyperactivity disorder. J Neuropsychol. 208;12(2):165-75. pubmed.gov. As cited in Clinical Implications of the Perception of Time in Attention Deficit Hyperactivity Disorder (ADHD): A Review. ncbi.nlm.nih.gov/pmc/articles/PMC6556068/

the time because our best intentions don't always line up with our irresponsible-looking actions.[58]

My very first date with my ex-husband was in Quebec City where we had met in a French language immersion class. Casey and I had agreed to meet in the Old City at a particular time. I was staying with a family outside of Vieux, Quebec, so I needed to take a bus into town. I got on the bus in what I thought would be plenty of time. However, the bus seemed to be going in a circuitous route, stopping every couple of blocks, and taking way longer than it should have to drive the 20 minutes into town. We didn't have cell phones yet, so I couldn't text Casey to let him know I was running late.

By the time we got to my stop in Vieux, Quebec, I was 30 minutes late for my first date with him. Casey was still sitting on the ground under a tree, and he immediately sprang up to greet me as I stepped off the bus. I felt so bad about keeping him waiting that long. "I'm sorry I'm late!" I apologized several times. And then, because I always have to defend my mess-ups and give an excuse, I said "I don't know how that happened! I got on the bus when I was supposed to, but it just took forever to get here, for some reason." He told me he had just been about to leave because he figured I wasn't going to show. He was glad I'd finally made it, and he pointed out that I'd gotten on the regular bus rather than on the express bus. That was why it had taken me so long.

---

[58] Paul, Jaclyn. "How It Really Feels to Be Time-Blind with ADHD." *ADHD Homestead.net*, 11 Apr. 2018, https://adhdhomestead.net/time-blindness-feels/.

Wait, there were two different buses? How was I supposed to know that?! When it comes to time perception and time management, we ADHD-ers are on the regular bus while everyone else seems to have taken the express bus. We aren't going to get wherever we're going quickly, but we will always have a story to tell.

20

Trouble with Procedural Memory

When adults are required to learn something, instead of taking "classes," we go to "trainings." At the end of these trainings, we are supposed to understand and be able to implement new skill sets. I always enter into trainings with a feeling of optimism. After all, the end result of this "training" is that *I will be trained.* How nice to know the trainers have it all under control and know exactly what I need to be able to do my job well.

Unfortunately, I don't think I've ever left a training feeling trained. Overwhelmed, maybe. Confused, irritated, far behind, and hopeless, perhaps. But not trained. Every "training" goes something like this:

Me (to coworker, noticing handouts being passed around and everyone typing on their computers): "What are we supposed to be doing?"

Coworker: "Just pull down the drop screen and then right click on the calendar page and scroll down and choose 'options' and input your data."

Me: "Oh, OK" (I pull down the drop screen) "What happens after the drop screen?"

Coworker: "Right-click."

Me: "Sure, OK." (trying to remember where to right-click)

Trainer (continues to go through steps):"So now you should be able to input all your data in the right fields." (People begin to leave)

Me (increasingly clinging to my coworker like a drowning person): "What does this handout say to do in step 7?"

Coworker: "You just hit "edit" at the top and then you can attach files and upload data."

Me: "Oh, right."

(Everyone leaves. I'm still on step 3. I feel like a child who can't go outside until she eats all her peas. I will never get to go outside again).

Thanks to leaky working memory, my ADHD brain can't put together much of a mental map, and that means that trying to make my way through a set of procedures is like having a limited cell data plan. If I were driving from point A to point B, I would put the address into Google maps and I'd get a full map showing the roads between me and my destination and the turns I needed to take. If I try to conjure up my own map, however, I might be able to manage picturing one or two roads that connect, but after that my map peters out. I don't have enough data available to me to be able to create the whole map in my head and work with it for any length of time. If I know where I'm going, I can trust that the map will create itself as I keep moving forward. It's as though the roads are actually being laid down as I drive. If I don't know where I'm going, or if I've only been somewhere once or twice, it's like a recurring dream of mine where I'm driving down the road in the pitch dark with no lights. I'm honestly just feeling my way through space and hoping that something will click.

With this limited cell data plan for a brain, when I'm given too many directions at once, they just peter off into blackness. Even if I can keep up, there's no way I can also manage to remember more than a couple of steps of the procedure that I'm supposedly being trained to do. I might be able to do it once, with lots of coaching and reminders, but I'll never be able to repeat the process on my own. I need time to write out each step in a way that I can understand. Those handouts with directions on them are written by people who don't think like I do. I need directions that make sense for me.

I'm much better in one-on-one training sessions because I have more control over the pace, and I can stop to write things down and ask questions. Those group trainings on how to use various databases and apps, how to upload and manipulate digital information, are just the worst. My anxiety level is so high going into them because I know I'm going to fail. I'm going to fall behind. I won't be able to control my frustration tolerance. I'll do or say something socially unacceptable in an effort to stay on track. I'll feel rejected or disrespected, and I'll slink out of there in shame, afraid to ask for help.

It's worth pointing out here again that women's and men's experience of ADHD differs in terms of how much internalized shame and feelings of low self esteem are attached to it. Dr. Ellen Litman, in her research on women and ADHD, says that "most women struggle with an internalized sense of impairment that affects their sense of self and qualitative life management skills." Perhaps because of our gender roles and fluctuating hormones, women with ADHD have a greater tendency towards self-doubt and self-harm. We anticipate criticism or rejection because of our inadequacies with time management, organization, motivation, and memory. We may feel shame because of our emotional reactivity, and therefore we internalize our feelings, censoring ourselves and refusing to reach out for support rather than risking inappropriate responses.[59]

Actually, hormones do seem to have a lot to do with it. Estrogen and progesterone have a marked effect on cognitive function. When they are high, ADHD symptoms abate; when they are low (leading up to monthly menstruation, or during

---

[59] Littman, Ellen, PhD. (March 3, 2022). Copyright © 1998 - 2023 WebMD LLC. All rights reserved. Women with ADHD: No More Suffering in Silence. Additudemag.com. https://www.additudemag.com/gender-differences-in-adhd-women-vs-men

and after menopause), cognitive function and ADHD symptoms worsen. It would stand to reason that our Rejection Sensitive Dysphoria worsens as well.

Remember the University of California-Berkeley longitudinal study I mentioned in Chapter 8 about the higher tendency of girls with ADHD towards suicidal thinking and behavior? Dr. Littman's research explains the reasons why. According to Littman's research,

> *Compared to men, women with ADHD perceive themselves as more impaired, and their experience of negative events as more painful. They are more likely to blame themselves for their difficulties, and feel lucky if things turn out well. They are more likely to struggle with low self-esteem and shame. It appears that women with ADHD are more vulnerable to their perceived failures in self-regulation than men.*

Thanks to hormonal fluctuations and differences in societal expectations and identity development, women may be hard-wired to perceive our ADHD weaknesses as "unworthiness." Littman writes,

> *Such hopelessness, combined with impulsivity, contributes to significantly more self-harm compared to men. Even more concerning is their much greater likelihood of suicidal thoughts and attempts. Recent population studies suggest that women with ADHD are*

> *more likely to die earlier of unnatural causes, especially due to accidents.*[60]

Well that's it, then, I'm done attending group trainings. They are obviously hazardous to my health.

Here's something funny, I actually thought my self-esteem was pretty high before I began writing this book. Sometimes it takes a whole lot of introspection, and especially forcing ourselves to remember and write out our stories, before we begin to be able to perceive ourselves more accurately. Especially for those of us whose working memory issues are particularly profound, it's critical that we maintain a written record of our life experiences. When Casey and I were going through our divorce, I wrote down as many stories as I could about things that had happened in our relationship and how each of us had acted. I referred back to those stories whenever I found myself suffering from intense feelings of rejection and failure. My written record of events helped me remember things more accurately and reminded me that it wasn't all my fault.

It's important for women, especially, to remember that our identities don't have to depend on what other people want us to do. If you're always focused on "what was I supposed to do, again?" then you aren't going to be able to make use of your own creative talents. You'll expend so much energy on trying to please people and on trying to mask your ADHD difficulties that you'll have none left over for creative self-

------

[60]Litman, Ellen. Women with ADHD: No more suffering in silence. Addictudemag.com. June 5, 2023.

expression and dazzling people with your impressive, out-of-the-box thinking.

Sometimes your perspective will scare people because it's not familiar to them and doesn't fit with their schema. As a result of their own discomfort, they may redouble their efforts to make you feel bad about yourself. I guarantee you this is an experience shared by the greatest inventors and forward-looking thinkers in history. People don't like what they can't understand, and they want you to fit into their mold. Step away from what you're "supposed" to do, and you'll discover that we are the musicians, actors, comedians, writers, inventors, entrepreneurs, and overall creative geniuses of the world. Let's try not to forget that.

21

Adulting with ADHD

Happy 21st chapter to you! Now that we've reached Chapter 21, we should have gained some emotional maturity, know-how, self-awareness, practical life experience, and goals for the future. They say we're adults by our 21st chapter, but "adulting" has been a little more difficult for us than for most. Since ADHD is a disorder of delayed development, I figure we should be on track with our 21 year old peers by the time we're, say, 85 or so.

We've been through a lot of heartbreak together, celebrated some important parts of our identities, and laughed at our foibles. Hopefully this book has allowed you to pinpoint your problem areas and helped you to understand the reasons behind some of your personality traits. Here's a helpful summary of some of the things we've learned:

- Anxiety and rigidity are bound up with stuck fear circuitry, the same fear feedback loop responsible for PTSD.
- Negativity and oppositional defiance are behavioral habits that become addictive because they stimulate our brains with neurochemicals we have trouble accessing. Once those neurochemicals are in business, we can cope better with our lives.
- We have a marked tendency towards addiction and even self-harm.
- Impatience, inner restlessness, impulsiveness, and emotional dysregulation (quick to anger, intense, overly talkative), are all aspects of hyperactivity, which happens when the brain doesn't have the optimum balance of dopamine, norepinephrine, and serotonin.
- hypersensitivity to the things around us (noises, movement, smells, textures) causes us to shift our attention around constantly and sometimes causes us to shut down altogether.
- hypersensitivity to perceived criticism (rejection sensitive dysphoria) is something that many people with ADHD and other disorders involving the executive functioning of the brain have in common.

- Our brains are wired to seek out interesting stimuli and novelty. We can sustain our attention for long periods at a time if something is interesting or new to us.
- We have a different relationship to time than our neurotypical peers, in part because of our leaky working memory that cannot hold a linear sequence of events in the mind's eye.
- We depend heavily upon the emotional centers of our brains to help us track time, to remember the past, and to take action in the present.
- We are motivated by high-stakes, imminent rewards and punishments, including our own anxiety about what will happen if we are late, or miss a deadline, or forget something important. If our anxiety is high enough, it can keep us on track (at a cost). We are not motivated by importance, time, rewards or consequences too far in the future.
- The world we live in is blurry. We can't piece out details and put them in order of importance or priority. We can't see where to begin and end.
- We may be highly empathetic and read people's emotions well, but in social settings we often lack self-awareness in the moment.
- In low-interest settings, we have a terrible time beginning, maintaining alertness, and following through.
- When it comes to task-shifting or employing a new approach to a task, we often get stuck.

- We are a mess of inconsistencies: we can be just as adaptable as we can be rigid and inflexible; we can be hyperfocused, anxious workaholics just as much as we can be inefficient time-wasters who can't hold down a job; we can be forgetful and selfish partners just as much as we can be attentive, doting, and thoughtful.

Thom Hartmann, in his book *Attention Deficit Disorder: A Different Perception*, theorizes that people with ADHD thrived for many thousands of years in nomadic, hunter-gatherer societies before the evolution of agricultural societies made some of our best ADHD traits moot.[61] We are the original cavemen who hunted with careful precision and hyperfocus, dodged danger, wandered far afield chasing after the best chances of survival, and found a cave to paint out our experiences on the walls.

Consider the ways in which we are constantly scanning our surroundings, our senses on high alert, or zeroing in on something of interest with precision focus. Indoors, or in sedentary positions, we are like trapped animals, restless and ill at ease, but outside and moving we feel much more ourselves. Fresh air and physical exertion from hiking, biking, swimming, and other outdoor sports helps us feel focused, peaceful, and "normal." I know that for me, one of my favorite things in the whole world is going for a hike and then sitting down somewhere outside to eat a simple and delicious snack.

---

[61] Hartmann, T. (1997). Attention Deficit Disorder: A Different Perception. Underwood Books.

Not long ago, I was hiking with Ben up in the mountains. We were walking and chatting. But my attention, thankfully, wasn't fully on Ben. I was idly looking around and down at my feet, unconsciously scanning my environment. As we walked, I suddenly became aware of a change in texture and color between the grass and something I was about to step on. Instead of putting my foot down on it, I instinctively jumped away. It was a rather large copperhead snake lying in the long grass! It stayed there placidly, its head erect, and we studied it from a safe distance.

Would someone without ADHD have noticed that snake? I have to wonder. Our "hunter/gatherer" brains serve us well in high-intensity situations with plenty of unexpected novelty and interesting things to act upon. We do well as emergency first responders, nurses, doctors, teachers, entrepreneurs, chefs, social workers, police officers, trainers, coaches, and doing anything we are passionate about that has lots of moving parts.

Not only are we hunters, but we are also artists, making sense of our world in creative ways – perhaps through music, painting, poetry, comedy, dance or other types of performance. We are quintessential impressionists, "feeling" each moment as a blur of colors, or shifting light, or movement and texture. We can be exceptionally good at improvisation. I listened to a Ted Talk once that was given by a neuroscientist on the topic of creativity. The neuroscientist explained what they saw on MRI scans of the brains of jazz musicians when the musicians were improvising. Interestingly, prefrontal cortex activity (the place of executive functions, those self-regulating inhibitory processes) was quite minimal. It seems as though the parts of the brain that control our behavior and give us the ability to self-monitor must be suppressed in order to allow for the spontaneous flow of creativity.

When we are unburdened by logic, fear, and self-consciousness, we become creative thinkers. We come up with surprising connections, brilliant big-picture ideas, and creative approaches to problems because our brains don't hone the firing of neurons for the purpose of executive functioning. We are less held back by what we already know to be true or practical. Our natural inclination towards uncensored brain activity leads to creative output! After all, what is innovation but a fearless and seemingly irrational approach that can lead to bold, new ideas?

Many businesses and organizations prize the very strengths we exhibit: creativity, energy, enthusiasm, innovative problem-solving. The trick to being able to utilize our innovative and novelty-energized gifts is to take over the controls. In situations where it's appropriate and useful to cultivate an impressionistic sense of the world, we can let that happen. But in situations where it's untenable, we must have ways and means to turn on other parts of our brains.

I haven't talked much about medications for ADHD, except to try to explain a little bit about how stimulants work. But now that we've come to the last chapter, I will tell you that stimulant medication allowed me to write this book. I generated ideas at all times of the day and night – in the car, on dog walks, in the bathtub, waiting in line at the store, awake at 4am… I came up with what I wanted to include in the book both while I was on and while I was off of medication. I captured those ideas in voice memos, on index cards, in notebooks, and, of course, on many, many scraps of paper. It was the medication, though, that gave me the clarity to be able to sit down and write out my thoughts in some sort of linear progression-- to take an incoherent jumble of ideas, feelings, metaphors, connections, and goals and make some sense out of it. The medication allowed me to reach the potential I knew I was capable of. I maintained the motivation, alertness, and planning needed to write a book!

Some people find that regular exercise, good habits, and structure are enough to help them manage their ADHD. I found that I couldn't even begin to manage my ADHD without the push the medication provides. Without the medication, my head is full of layer upon layer of ideas, and plans, and desires. But none of them bubbles up to the surface long enough to get accomplished. With the medication, I can see the separate pieces of things, put them in a sensible order, and take action more easily. I can make myself do things that need to get done. I can see the trees for the forest. For me, medication shifts my perspective so I can hold onto the things I want to hold onto and let go of the things I don't.

You know how you can be gazing at clouds and they begin to take on a shape that you recognize? Out of the fluff, you suddenly see something tangible that means something specific to you? That's what medication does for me. It gives the formless clouds shape and meaning. My reality literally shifts as I begin to see things more clearly. I wrote this poem about it:

Clouds are a study
in perspective.
What you think is true
changes with the wind--
so slowly, you do not see
the elephant wings
coming.

Your job is to allow
the lizard to bite
its own back.
Allow the swan's neck
to heal.

It will probably break
again,
but only to become
something
new.

If we are to move forward, we must change our
perspective by finding ways to trick our brains into forming
tangible images we can work with. We must be ready to pounce
on those moments of focus before they melt away. We must
have resources to get them back again when they disappear. We
have lived with a chronic, low-level sense of dread that the
universe will erupt into chaos at any moment. But now it's time
for an origin story. In many origin stories of different cultures,

some event takes place that creates shape and meaning from formless darkness and that manages, somehow, to stem the potential chaos and create order that allows life to flourish. We can create that order, and we can control the chaos. Now that we have a fuller understanding of our issues (and as one of my ADHD friends says "Even my issues have issues"), we "got this."

I've had a recurring dream over the past few years where I am walking through what my brain knows to be my own house (though I don't recognize it as my actual house). As I'm going through the rooms, I come to a door that I never noticed before. I open the door, and there's a huge bonus room behind it. I'm thrilled because suddenly I have all this extra space I didn't know I had in my house. I start thinking about all the possible ways I might be able to use it--as an office? a music room? a game room? a library? I think about the value this room will add to my house, now that I know it's here. I walk into the empty space and begin dancing around. It's a tremendous discovery, and I can't wait to turn it into something fantastic.

I think this extra room is a part of my brain that's been hidden from me for a long, long time. Suddenly, there's a door and it's accessible. The door began to materialize after I got diagnosed with ADHD and sought understanding and help. If you need some direction for how to access your own potential "bonus room," here are my recommended steps:

1. Find a psychologist in your area who specializes in adult ADHD testing if you suspect you (or a loved one) has ADHD but hasn't been diagnosed.

2. Gain a thorough understanding of how your brain works and acknowledge the ways ADHD has tripped you up in life. (If you've read this book, then you're well on your way)! You might also read through the fabulous articles from additudemag.com.

3. Find a support group in your area such as chadd.org (children and adults with attention deficit/hyperactivity disorder)

4. Learn about the various stimulant and non stimulant medications for ADHD and consider their risks and benefits to you. Dr. Russell Barkley, Savior of the Scattered, devotes a chapter to medication in his book Taking Charge of Adult ADHD, and he also details strategies for "adulting" successfully.

5. Find a good therapist who can address your specific behavior patterns and thinking habits through cognitive behavioral therapy or dialectical behavior therapy.

6. Consider working with a certified ADHD coach to help you with accountability, and to teach you practical strategies for externalizing those things you don't internalize well. "Externalizing" simply means depending on external cues and tools for organizing, keeping track of time, remembering important things, etc, rather than trying to keep everything in your head.

7. Find a friend at work who is good at the things you're not, and see if they'd be willing to help you when you need it.

8. Listen to ADHD podcasts such as the ones that are part of the ADHD ReWired network for tips and tricks to make your ADHD brain work for you.

I know that seems like a lot of steps. It's easy to get sidetracked and to give up, but you've come this far already. Take the next step towards discovering the door that's been there all along. You know you want to see what that room behind it can become.

I'll let you in on a little secret, it's taken me not one, but four summer vacations to finish this book. Not only that, but after teaching through the worst year of the Covid-19 pandemic, I resigned. I realized that I wanted to work from home, I wanted to write more, and I wanted to pursue a dream I had never allowed myself to think was possible. The "bonus room" from my dream that I've had all along turned out to be my home office. It is, in fact, the perfect size and shape for a recording studio. I built acoustic panels for the walls and added sound absorption all over the small room. I bought professional equipment and applied myself to training and practice in a way only an ADHD-er with a high interest can. After my last summer vacation, once this book was finished, I transformed myself from a teacher to a full-time voice over actor and writer. And this is the same person whose husband once accused her of having "no ambition." You and I both know that the more interested we are, the more support and encouragement we have, and the less squashed we are by demands from linear thinkers or systems, the more we thrive.

We just have to figure out how to make our own way. It is the problem-solving task of a lifetime, but I promise you we are equal to the task. I am rooting for you, or for your loved one who is struggling. You got this!

And now I'd like to send a copy of this book to show my appreciation to the nice man who diagnosed me. If I could just remember his name! Dr. So-and-So changed my life. I hope I've helped change yours.

This is only the beginning...

Bibliography

ADDitude Magazine. Copyright 1998-2023 All rights reserved. https://www.ADDitudemag.com

Amen, Daniel. as cited in Pera, Gina. *Is it You, Me, or Adult ADD?* pg. 94.

Albajara Sáenz, A., Septier, M., Van Schuerbeek, P. et al. "ADHD and ASD: Distinct Brain Patterns of Inhibition Related Activation?" *Translational Psychiatry.* 2020, vol. 10, article 24. https://doi.org/10.1038/s41398-020-0707-z

Arabi, Shahida. *Power: Surviving and Thriving After Narcissistic Abuse: a Collection of Essays on Malignant Narcissism and Recovery from Emotional Abuse.* Thought Catalog Books, ed. 2017.

Arnsten AF. Stress "Signaling Pathways That Impair Prefrontal Cortex Structure and Function." *Nature Reviews Neuroscience.* Jun 2009, vol. 10 iss. 6, pp. 410-422. doi: 10.1038/nrn2648.

Austin, Margaret, PhD. *Gulfbend.org.* n.d. 22 April 2021. https://www.gulfbend.org/poc/view_doc.php?type=doc&id=13861.

Bancos, I. (Ed.). (2022, January 24). Copyright © 2023 Endocrine Society. All rights reserved. Adrenal Hormones. Endocrine.org. https://www.endocrine.org/patient-engagement/endocrine-library/hormones- and-endocrinefunction/adrenal-hormones/

Barkley, Russell, Benton, Christine. *Taking Charge of Adult ADHD: Proven Strategies to Succeed at Work, at Home, and in Relationships.* The Guilford Press, 2022.

Barkley, Russell, Fischer Mariellen. "Hyperactive Child Syndrome and Estimated Life Expectancy at Young Adult Follow-Up: The Role of ADHD Persistence and Other Potential Predictors." *Journal of Attention Disorders.* Sage Journals. Jul. 2019, vol. 23, iss. 9, pp. 907-923. https://journals.sagepub.com/

Barkley, Russell. "How ADHD Shortens Life Expectancy. What Parents and Doctors Need to Know to Take Action." Webinar. ADDitudemag.com. January 29, 2019.

Barkley, Russell. *Fact Sheet: Attention Deficit Hyperactivity Disorder (ADHD) Topics.* Russellbarkley.org

Broadbent , Elizabeth. "ADHD, Women, and the Danger of Emotional Withdrawal." *ADDitudemag.com*, 3 Mar. 2022. https://www.ADDitudemag.com/adhd-emotional-withdrawal-rejection-sensitivity-women/

Clinical Implications of the Perception of Time in Attention Deficit Hyperactivity Disorder (ADHD): A Review. https://ncbi.nlm.nih.gov/pmc/articles/PMC6556068/

American Psychiatric Association. Criteria for Attention-Deficit/Hyperactivity Disorder (ADHD). *Diagnostic and Statistical Manual of Mental Disorders.* 5th ed., text rev. 2022

Dodson, William. "Secrets of the ADHD Brain: Why We Think, Act, and Feel the Way We Do." *ADDitude Magazine.* New Hope Media, New York, NY. 2016. Pg. 11

Durall, John K. "Toward an Understanding of ADHD: A Developmental Delay in Self-Control." *Camping Magazine,* vol.72, no.1, p38-41 Jan./Feb. 1999. American Camp Association. https://www.acacamps.org.

Hallowell, E.M., Ratey, J.J. *Driven to Distraction: Recognizing and Coping with Attention Deficit Disorder from Childhood through Adulthood.* Simon & Schuster, New York, 2011.

Hallowell, E.M. "In Praise of the ADHD Funny Bone." ADDitudemag.com. 11 Apr. 2022, https://www.ADDitudemag.com/how-to-be-funny-adult-adhd.

Hartmann, Thom. *Attention Deficit Disorder: A Different Perception.* Underwood. 2nd. ed., 1997.

Hinshaw, S.P., Carte, E.T., Fan, D., Jassy, J.S. & Owens, E.B. "Neuropsycholological Functioning of Girls with Attention Deficit/Hyperactivity Disorder Followed Prospectively into Adolescence: Evidence for Continuing Deficits?" *Neuropsychology,* vol. 21, 2007, pp. 263-73.

Hinshaw, S.P., Owens, E.B., Sami, N., Fargeon, S. "Prospective Follow-up of Girls with Attention-Deficit/Hyperactivity Disorder into Adolescence: Evidence for Continuing Cross-Domain Impairment." *Journal of Consulting and Clinical Psychology,* vol. 74, 2006, pp. 489-499.

The Lancet. "People with ADHD are Twice as Likely to Die Prematurely, Often Due to Accidents." ScienceDaily. https://www.sciencedaily.com/releases/2015/02/150225205834.htm

Litz, A. Walton, and Christopher MacGowan, editors. *The Collected Poems of William Carlos Williams*. Reprint, vol. 1, New Directions, 1991.

Littman, Ellen. *What the ADHD Brain Wants – and Why*. 2014, https://Drellenlittman.com.

Littman, Ellen, Ph.D. "Never Enough? Why ADHD Brains Crave Stimulation." 18 May 2022, https://ADDitudemag.com.

Litman, Ellen, Ph.D. "Women with ADHD: No More Suffering in Silence." 3 Mar. 2022, https://ADDitudemag.com.

Nadeau, K.G. Ph.D., Littman, E.B. Ph.D., Quinn, P.O. MD. Nadeau. *Understanding Girls with ADHD: How They Feel and Why They Do What They Do*. 2nd ed., Advantage Books, 2015. "Forward." Hinshaw, S. Ph.D. pg. xvii

National Center for Learning Disabilities. *Executive Function 101*. 2013, National Center for Learning Disabilities, Inc. As cited in https://edrevsf.org. .

Nazari, M.A., Mirloo, M.M., Rezaei, M., Sotanlou, M. "Emotional Stimuli Facilitate Time Perception in Children with Attention-Deficit/Hyperactivity Disorder." *Journal of Neuropsychology*, vol. 12, no. 2, June 2018, pp. 165–75. pubmed.gov. Cited in Clinical Implications of the Perception of Time in Attention Deficit Hyperactivity Disorder (ADHD): A Review.ncbi.nlm.nih.gov/pmc/articles/PMC6556068/

Paul, Jaclyn. "How It Really Feels to Be Time-Blind with ADHD." *ADHD Homestead.net*. 11 Apr. 2018. https://adhdhomestead.net/time-blindness-feels/.

Pera, Gina. *Is It You, Me, or Adult A.D.D? Stopping the Roller Coaster When Someone You Love Has Attention Deficit Disorder*. 1201 Alarm Press, 2008.

Ptacek, R., Weissenberger, S., Braaten, E., Klicperova -Baker, M., Goetz, M., Raboch, J., Vnukova, M., Stefano, G.B. "Clinical Implications of the Perception of Time in Attention Deficit Hyperactivity Disorder (ADHD): A Review." *Medical Science Monitor*. 26 May 2019,vol. 25, pp.3918-3924. doi: 10.12659/MSM.914225. PMID: 31129679; PMCID: PMC65560

Radboud University Nijmegen Medical Centre. "Brain differences in ADHD." *ScienceDaily*. https://www.sciencedaily.com/releases/2017/02/170216105919.htm.

Roberts, Kevin. *Movers Dreamers and Risk-Takers: Unlocking the Power of ADHD*. Hazelden, 2012.

Rodkey, Geoff. *The Tapper Twins Tear up New York*. Little, Brown, 2016.

Rogers, F., & Head, B. "Songs and Music from Mister Rogers' Neighborhood." In Mister Rogers Talks With Parent (pp. 282–285). Song. Berkley Books, 1983, New York by arrangement with Family Communications, Inc.

Shaw P, Lurch J, Greenstein D, Sharp W, Clasen L, Evans A, et al. "Longitudinal Mapping of Cortical Thickness and Clinical Outcome in Children and Adolescents with Attention-Deficit/Hyperactivity Disorder." *Archives of General Psychiatry*, vol. 63, 2006, pp. 540–49.
As cited in Vaidya, Chandan J. "Neurodevelopmental Abnormalities in ADHD."

Sigler, Eunice. "ADHD Looks Different in Women. Here's How – and Why." *ADDitude Inside the ADHD Mind*, 3 Mar. 2022, https://www.ADDitudemag.com.

Spencer, A.E., Marin, M.F, Milad, M.R., et al. "Abnormal Fear Circuitry in Attention Deficit Hyperactivity Disorder: A Controlled Magnetic Resonance Imaging Study." *Psychiatry Research: Neuroimaging*, no. 262, 10 Feb. 2017, pp. 55–62, https://ADDitudemag.com/adhd-ptsd-fear-circuit-deficits/.

Understood Team. "Why Some Kids Play the 'Class Clown.'" *Understood*, https://www.understood.org/.

Vaidya , C.J. "Neurodevelopmental Abnormalities in ADHD." *Current Topics in Behavioral Neurosciences*, vol. 9, pp. 49–66, https://www.ncbi.nim/nih.gov/pmc/articles/PMC3329889.

Villines, Zawn. "What Does Neurotypical, Neurodivergent, and Neurodiverse Mean?" Medical News Today, 3 Feb. 2022, https://www.medicalnewstoday.com/

Wanderwisdom.com "How to Return Lava Rocks to Hawaii
    https://www.wanderwisdom.com/travel-
    destinations/How-to- Return-Lava-Rocks-to-Hawaii

Young, S., Moss, D., Sedgwick, O., Fridman, M., Hodgkins, P. "A
    Meta-Analysis of the Prevalence of Attention Deficit
    Hyperactivity Disorder in Incarcerated Populations."
    Psychological Medicine, vol. 45, no. 2, Jan. 2015,
    pp. 247–58.

www.ingramcontent.com/pod-product-compliance
Lightning Source LLC
Chambersburg PA
CBHW020153090426
42734CB00008B/804